More Praise for *One Second Ahead*

"Rasmus Hougaard and The Potential Project have cleverly combined two hot topics in today's work life: mindfulness and working more effectively. You can find thousands of useful books on both topics, but Rasmus has gone one step further. Putting together a great variety of work techniques with mindfulness creates an extremely powerful toolset for any professional who not only wants more from him/herself, but is also interested in own self's wellbeing."

—Jouni Torunen, HR Director, Nokia

"*One Second Ahead* is a major contribution to bringing not only more sanity and mindfulness at the work place but also a more caring and open-minded attitude in all walks of life. Highly recommended."

—Matthieu Ricard, humanitarian and Buddhist monk, author of *Altruism: How Compassion Can Change Your Life and the World.*

"In *One Second Ahead* Rasmus Hougaard ingeniously applies time-tested ancient methods of mental training to practical day-to-day circumstances that are regularly encountered in the business world. This book is bound to be of much practical benefit to all those who seek a more satisfying, creative, and fulfilling way of life within their professional and personal relationships."

—B. Alan Wallace, Ph.D. Author of bestseller *The Attention Revolution* and President, Santa Barbara Institute for Consciousness Studies

"Like many other busy professionals we at Herbert Smith Freehills face the same demands of long working hours, increasing commercial complexity, and competing distractions for our attention and for our effort. To be a globally elite law firm, we need to be focused, crystal clear in our thinking and highly effective. This book distils the essence of the Potential Project's mindfulness program. If you put into action what you learn here, particularly the daily practice, then I am sure you will gain a greater sense of who you are, and a sense of calm and perspective that will enable you to be the best person you can be at work and at home."

—Murray Paterson, Head of Capability Development, Herbert Smith Freehills, Australia

"A mindful organization is an organization where our leaders and employees do the right things—not just things. Through the program behind this book, we have gradually become a mindful organization"

—Former CIO, Carlsberg, Kenneth Egelund Schmidt

"Rasmus Hougard, Jacqueline Carter and Gillian Coutts have skillfully woven an elegant set of mindfulness tools and strategies that any professional can implement. This is a fantastic foundation for a more mindful workplace and life."

—Jeremy Hunter, PhD, Associate Professor of Practice Peter F. Drucker and Masatoshi Ito Graduate School of Management

"In our organization we have implemented the program of mindfulness and after completing the program the stress level have decreased significantly and our employees are more focused. But the techniques outlined in *One Second Ahead* are not just for work situations, they are also highly valuable in all kind of scenario—both professional and private. The book will give you better and more mindful interactions with everyone you meet."

—Hans Brobäck, Human Resources Director, Roche

"Since undertaking mindfulness training, I have been pleasantly surprised by the positive impact the training has had on my creativity. By choosing to focus on only one task at a time, I engage in more useful conversations with my colleagues and have also found that my enhanced concentration has significantly improved my overall creative output."

—Nick Foley, President SE Asia Pacific & Japan, Landor

"The pace and complexity in today's organizations affects all co-workers and leaders in all aspects. Especially when the boundaries between work and "life" becomes more and more interlinked. The decision to use CBMT as a tool in order to decrease stress levels in our organization turned out to be a real game changer for our co-workers. I can highly recommend this book because it captures all the benefits with working with CBMT in all kinds of organizations. The tone of voice is fact-driven and combines real examples from organizations backed up with theories and scientific studies."

—Henrik Scheutz, Function Manager HR Service Centre, IKEA AB

One Second Ahead

Enhance Your Performance at Work with Mindfulness

Rasmus Hougaard
Jacqueline Carter
Gillian Coutts

ONE SECOND AHEAD

First published 2016 by
PALGRAVE MACMILLAN

The authors have asserted their rights to be identified as the authors of this work in accordance with the Copyright, Designs and Patents Act 1988.

Palgrave Macmillan in the UK is an imprint of Macmillan Publishers Limited, registered in England, company number 785998, of Houndmills, Basingstoke, Hampshire, RG21 6XS.

Palgrave Macmillan in the US is a division of Nature America, Inc., One New York Plaza, Suite 4500, New York, NY 10004-1562.

Palgrave Macmillan is the global academic imprint of the above companies and has companies and representatives throughout the world.

Hardback ISBN: 978-1-137-55190-0
E-PUB ISBN: 978-1-137-55191-7
E-PDF ISBN: 978-1-137-55192-4
DOI: 10.1057/9781137551924

Distribution in the UK, Europe and the rest of the world is by Palgrave Macmillan®, a division of Macmillan Publishers Limited, registered in England, company number 785998, of Houndmills, Basingstoke, Hampshire RG21 6XS.

Library of Congress Cataloging-in-Publication Data

Hougaard, Rasmus.
    One second ahead : enhance your performance at work with mindfulness / Rasmus Hougaard, Jacqueline Carter, Gillian Coutts.
        pages cm
    Includes bibliographical references and index.
    ISBN 978-1-137-55190-0 (alk. paper)
        1. Mental efficiency. 2. Performance—Psychological aspects.
    3. Work—Psychological aspects. I. Coutts, Gillian. II. Title.
BF632.H69 2015
158.7—dc23   2015019343

A catalogue record of the book is available from the British Library.

Printed in the United States of America.

Contents

Foreword to *One Second Ahead*

To be honest, I am probably the last person one might expect to write a foreword to a book on mindfulness, but two years ago, I had a series of profound insights and realizations that changed my perspective in a significant way.

First, I realized my brain was full—full with all of the things associated with living a high-pressure, fast-paced, demanding life. Second, I realized that I essentially had assumed that having a "full brain" was unavoidable and that if I wanted to be a successful leader in one of the world's largest consulting, technology, and outsourcing firms, it was simply part of the "package."

However, I discovered another way of working and being that not only freed up brain capacity but also made me more effective, more creative, less stressed, and most probably more kind. These realizations have inspired me to write this foreword.

Strange as it may sound, I don't really like to "practice" mindfulness. Sitting still for ten minutes a day is a stretch for me, but I have found that if I do, the quality of my leadership, my work, and my private life improves.

Let me take you back to where this all began for me. For a number of years, I have led an extremely dedicated and high-performing SWAT team located across Europe, Africa, and Latin America. This team is a small but highly specialized group designed to lead and deliver our most complex and challenging engagements for some of the largest companies globally. We travel extensively, work very long hours, and manage extremely complex business challenges with our most demanding clients. It is great and rewarding work, but there can be a cost.

When you add today's "always-on" technology, constant data overload, and extreme time pressure to the work that we do, even the best, brightest, most mentally strong and talented people are sometimes unable to cope. Stress can be a debilitating illness, and a specific event changed my perspective. I had not seen it coming, and I was stunned.

This drove me to search for tools for enhancing *sustainable* performance, tools that could help my people and me do the work we love, while performing at the highest level, but without sacrificing well-being and balance in life.

The word mindfulness kept coming up, but at first it seemed far too "fluffy" and "soft" to me, and I had a belief that that bringing mindfulness into an organization could be close to a reputation suicide. There would be skeptics who saw mindfulness as soft and flaky, and those who would demand a "business case." There would be the "wise ones" who would not see the need to change. Above all, there would be the action addicts who would equate the idea of slowing down with some form of death.

By chance, I came in contact with Rasmus Hougaard and heard of his global team of trainers and consultants and their impressive track record of great results with large companies around the world. Rasmus had spent years with researchers, business leaders, and mindfulness masters to create their program, and, contrary to my reservations, it spoke directly to the business focus of a fast-paced organization like my own.

Working together, we designed a program tailored for my team and our work environment. The results have been outstanding: 30 percent increase in focus, 23 percent increase in effective prioritization, 25 percent decrease in unproductive multitasking, 30 percent increase in sleep quality, 31 percent increased memory, and 19 percent decrease in mental tiredness and stress, to mention a few.

It is a great pleasure for me to recommend this book to you. I hope you will try out the work applications and mental strategies of mindfulness for yourself. They have made a huge difference in my work, leadership, and private life, as well as for the people on my team. I am convinced it can do the same for you.

ROBERT STEMBRIDGE,
Managing Director, Accenture Technology.

Introduction

It all started with a failure.

It was early 2005, and for the first time I had the opportunity to introduce mindfulness into a corporation. I had already practiced mindfulness for more than a decade and knew how it provided me with the focus and clarity to be more effective in my work.

Now, for the first time, I had the opportunity to give the gift of mindfulness to the staff and leaders of a division of a European professional services company.

For weeks I had planned the day. I was ready. I was passionate. From the morning up to lunch, I told stories, gave instructions, and put them to the practice. I was excited and certain they would be too.

But I was wrong. Badly wrong. After lunch, I was ready to continue— power packed and inspired. The group was not. They did not come back from lunch.

That was a tough moment for me—but it became a pivotal day. I realized how naive I had been, trying to bring something very personal into a professional context. Clearly, I had not connected the dots between mindfulness and work, between moment-by-moment awareness and success in the office. Convinced of the benefits of combining mindfulness and work life, I committed myself to finding a way to bridge the gap.

The book you are reading now is the result of that quest.

* * *

Work life has changed radically over the past few decades. People used to be able to focus their full attention on each and every task. Now they attempt to concentrate on work while dealing with a constant stream of text messages, e-mails, phone calls, meetings, and deadlines. Faced with a relentless flood of information and distractions, our brains try to process everything at once. In other words, we try to multitask.

But researchers have shown that multitasking is the worst possible reaction to information overload. According to a McKinsey & Company report, multitasking actually "makes human beings less productive, less creative, and less able to make good decisions."[1] In fact, numerous studies have found that modern office life is transforming competent professionals into frenzied underachievers.[2]

This should not be too much of a surprise. Many of us are under constant pressure, are always on, experience information overload, and work in highly distracting environments. I call it the PAID reality.

Figure I.1   The PAID reality.

As a result of the mind's natural tendency to wander and the PAID reality, you may not be able to pay attention long enough to read the rest of this introduction. Most likely, before you get to the last page, your mind will have wandered off to whatever you need to do next. Nowadays, due to the PAID reality, we are gradually losing our ability to manage our attention.

Are we destined to have minds that constantly wander, remain inattentive, and lose focus?

Thankfully, the answer is no. It is actually possible to train the brain to respond differently to today's constant interruptions through the practice of mindfulness.

Simply put, at its introductory level, mindfulness means trained attention. Based on thousands of years of practice, mindfulness techniques enable people to manage their attention, improve their awareness, and sharpen their focus and clarity.

One Second Ahead is about applying mindfulness techniques to daily work life. Based on a program in corporate mindfulness designed through our work in The Potential Project, this book provides real-world examples and lessons from organizations that have implemented mindfulness on a large scale. Thoroughly tested in a diverse range of industries in North America, Europe, Asia, and Australia, this program has resulted in measurable increases in productivity, effectiveness, job satisfaction, and much more.

In building this program, I brought together business leaders, researchers, and mindfulness masters to help develop a way to bridge mindfulness and work. After years of development, this program has been implemented by companies like Microsoft, Accenture, Roche, Nike, American Express, General Electric, Citrix, Google, Sony, Société Générale, KLM, IKEA, Royal Bank of Canada, Ogilvy, Carlsberg, and many more. Evaluated by third-party researchers, the quantitative results of this training include increased focus and effectiveness, as well as enhanced quality of life, reduced stress, and better well-being.

On an individual level, the program has helped people quickly and easily learn how to improve efficiency and increase self-control. For many of them, this has resulted in a distinct one-second edge in critical decision-making. Why one second? In today's business environment, one second is a quantifiable advantage.

"Speed wins," we often say. As human beings, we want information now; we want to take action in the moment. Whenever we are given a choice, we will opt for a service that delivers faster than the competition. There is a reason Google posts its search times. There is a reason we are increasingly turning to analytical tools like big data for near instantaneous glimpses at the information that drives our businesses.

One second matters.

So much so that today we talk of the "speed of business." How fast is that? A millisecond advantage on Wall Street has been estimated to be worth $20 billion a year.

And from a cognitive perspective, being one second ahead provides a clear edge in effectiveness and productivity. It offers the space and freedom to choose your distractions and direct your mental energy. We cannot always control what happens in our lives, but we can deliberately and thoughtfully choose our responses to those events.

Viktor Frankl, who survived a Nazi concentration camp, wrote, "Between stimulus and response there is a space. In that space is our power to choose our response. In our response lies our growth and our freedom."[3] Despite extreme conditions, he managed to choose his response rather than be a victim of his own reactivity.

This book gives you that freedom in the office or the boardroom, during a sales call or a high-stakes presentation.

To be clear, these techniques—as well as the practice of mindfulness itself—are not solely about making more money or accelerating a career. There is a bigger, more important purpose of mindfulness.

After my big failure ten years ago, the first organization that invited me to bring in corporate-based mindfulness training was the largest insurance company in Scandinavia. Thomas, the sales director of the company, sponsored the program. He initiated the program hoping to improve focus and effectiveness for himself and his staff. He experienced that happening—and he also experienced something else. Something much more significant.

He shared it with his department and me one month into the program. His words have stuck with me ever since. He said, "I have noticed that we are all becoming more effective and productive, and for this I am glad. But I'm also experiencing something more important. I feel like we're becoming better human beings, kinder, gentler and happier."

In the end, this is what mindfulness is about: being our best selves and realizing more of our potential in everyday life. People who are more focused, clear minded, and kind make for better organizations. And many better organizations make for a better world. Think of a world in which improving performance goes hand in hand with increasing kindness. And a world in which kindness is valued as much as efficiency and effectiveness, as much as revenue per share or operating cash flow.

It may sound overly optimistic, but I see it happening every day in the many organizations we serve around the globe.

* * *

Designed for busy professionals looking for a new way of working within high-stress, high-paced conditions, *One Second Ahead* has been written as a very practical, how-to guide. It includes research-tested tools that have been used successfully by some of today's most respected global brands.

Although the book will be of great interest to individuals in leadership roles, it has been developed to be highly relevant and applicable for people at all levels of an organization. Offering small, bite-sized techniques, the book tackles the most persistent inefficiencies and problems in the workday, such as e-mail, meetings, priorities, and planning. Each of these techniques is self-contained and easily implemented, providing readers with immediate results.

One Second Ahead draws from the wisdom and methods of a several-thousand-year-old tradition that today is known as mindfulness. While mindfulness has deep roots, its appearance in the broader culture is a more recent development. Despite the media's trumpeting of the benefits of mindfulness, however, the vast majority of people have not made mindfulness part of their daily lives and do not even know where to begin.

This book aims to change that by starting where busy people—like you—need immediate assistance: with the daily tasks that sap energy and reduce productivity. Once you have experienced success with these tasks, you can explore deeper mindfulness interventions that address the development of mental qualities such as presence, patience, kindness, and acceptance. From there, it is an easy step to transforming your life through the regular practice of mindfulness and its core tenets: sharp focus and open awareness.

The first part of the book examines mindfulness in a work-based context. This part opens with a chapter that lays the foundation for the concept of mindfulness, examines both its benefits and the data supporting its efficacy, and provides the most basic understanding necessary to succeed with the work-based techniques that follow. Divided into 16 concise modules, the techniques themselves are designed to be easily applied to daily work tasks. Integrating mindfulness into the core elements of work life, each of these techniques is intended to give you immediate benefits in productivity and performance.

In the next part, *One Second Ahead* outlines strategies for replacing negative thought patterns that could prevent you from achieving your full potential. The mental strategies in this section help rewire the brain by cultivating powerful mind qualities, as noted above. Rewiring, or retraining, the brain in this way will help you respond mindfully to unforeseen problems that crop up in the workplace, rather than reverting to negative, unhelpful habits.

Part 3 of the book offers a comprehensive look at the two foundational practices of mindfulness training: sharp focus and open awareness. Together, these two forms of training help develop a balanced and high-performing mind. Once you reach this level of understanding and commitment, you will find your ability to stay focused, aware, and mindful to be exponentially improved. You will also better understand how to apply mindfulness outside the office, experiencing greater peace and well-being in all aspects of your life.

If you want to take your training deeper and experience the full range of benefits that mindfulness offers, the last chapter in Part 3 includes a training plan for systematically implementing mindfulness on a day-to-day basis. Along with this plan, the chapter answers common questions about the daily practice of mindfulness—the how, when, and where. The chapter then concludes by discussing how mindfulness can be introduced into an organization. This includes advice and tips on how to start an organization-wide program based on experience with hundreds of companies that have successfully incorporate corporate-based mindfulness training.

Each of these parts focuses on providing you with readily applicable skills, as well as increased clarity and insight. At its core, this is a practical resource: one that delivers immediate results. But it is also an inspiring guide to working, thinking, and living better.

I have organized this book in such a way that you will have the opportunity to experience the benefits of mindfulness straight away. Although practice before theory may seem contradictory, very simply, in my experience, busy people are keen to get tools that can immediately help them in their day-to-day work life. This is a common criticism of books on mindfulness: too much mysticism and theory before the basic helpful, prescriptive information is reached. With this structure, I put the most immediate, practical, information up front. Once you experience success in the daily tasks that define your work day, my hope is you will look to embrace the broader implications of mindfulness and deepen your understanding of its application.

To help with this evolution, I have incorporated a number of special features and practical tools throughout the book, including

- Tools and techniques for implementing mindfulness at work to enhance focus, clarity and results
- Guidelines and reflections to change how you think about people and things in the workplace towards being more calm, clear-minded, creative and kind
- Simple yet detailed step-by-step instructions for systematic mindfulness training
- Vignettes and real-world stories to help illustrate key lessons and stimulate thought
- Guidelines for a 10-minute-per-day mindfulness program guaranteed to reshape your life both at work and at home
- A link to a training app that will enhance your learning and training

This book is inspired by the thousands of people who have used these techniques and strategies and started daily mindfulness training. Hearing their stories of personal transformation and success is the main reason why I wrote this book—to share these methods with a wider audience. In these pages, I will share some of their stories with you. Please note that all of the stories are real, although some of the names have been changed to respect privacy.

Although there is a logical progression throughout *One Second Ahead*, it is also designed so that you can pick and choose the sections that are of most interest to you. This means you can jump from Part to Part or Technique to Strategy and pull out what you need, when you need it.

This book is written from a singular point of view. However, it includes the collective insights, wisdoms and experiences of myself, my co-authors and our colleagues at The Potential Project. Therefore, when you read "I" know that it is a reflection of a collaborative effort to bring the benefits of mindfulness to workplaces around the globe.

For example, if you picked up the book because you are curious about how mindfulness can be applied to everyday work life, start with Part 1. However, if you want to dive right into more advanced mindfulness training, you can jump to Part 3. If you are in a leadership role and planning to introduce a mindfulness program to your peers and reports, you may want to go straight to the second half of the final chapter.

Regardless of how you choose to use this book, I hope it will be of long-lasting benefit to you. By practicing the book's methods only a few minutes a day, you can develop more effective mental habits, allowing you to thrive in even the most competitive, high-pressure situations. Most important, however, *One Second Ahead* is intended to empower you—and busy people like you—by providing a road map to improving performance through greater focus, awareness and clarity of mind.

PART I

Workplace Techniques

With the rise of the Internet and the growth of mobile devices, how and where we work has shifted. We no longer need to go to work—work comes to us. Even if we do go into the office every day, work-based problems can find us night or day, in a restaurant or at the ballpark.

Over thousands of years, however, our brains have evolved to handle a very different kind of work. Humans historically survived through physical labor as hunters, farmers, and even for a period, as industrial workers. During this time, people were self-sufficient and tasks were clear: kill an animal, gather firewood, plow a field. Even on the production lines of Henry Ford and Frederick Taylor, the work was well defined—hammer x number of bolts in y hours.

In all of these cases, there was a singular focus to the work and a clear demarcation between field, forest, factory floor, and home. This means our brains aren't naturally wired to operate effectively in our new reality. To help visualize the shift, see Figure PI.1.

Today's information-driven work environment is frequently hectic and often ambiguous, with the lines between work and home becoming more and more blurred by each new productivity app. It's not hugely surprising, then, that the World Health Organization predicts work-related stress, burnout, and depression to be among the world's most prevalent diseases by 2020, joining perpetual killers like stroke and diabetes.[1]

At the very least, we face a challenge. On the one hand, we have an exciting, stimulating, and complex work life. It's fast paced, dynamic,

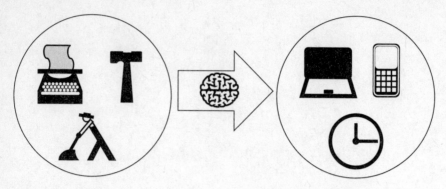

Figure PI.1 Work-life has changed.

and filled with possibility. On the other hand, we have a brain built for simpler times. Thankfully, there are things we can do to better manage the challenges of today's work life to stay one second ahead of the demands and responsibilities of our information-laden existence.

Part I of the book examines different techniques designed to help you face today's fast-paced reality with energy, enthusiasm, and balance. Presented as bite-sized, self-contained modules short enough to read during your commute or lunch break, each of the following 16 Techniques deals with ways to optimize your mental resources and well-being while facing specific challenges in the workplace. The more techniques you implement in a meaningful way, the greater benefit they'll be to you and the people you work with.

To lay the necessary foundation for applying these Techniques, Part I opens with a concise chapter that defines mindfulness, examines both its benefits and the data supporting its efficacy, and explains the most basic skills needed to implement mindfulness in an office environment.

Bear in mind, though, these techniques are just one very practical facet of the much bigger and broader tradition of mindfulness. The real key to mindfulness and a mindful life is in the daily practice, as defined and presented in Part III. My sincere hope is that once you experience success with these quick, hands-on workplace techniques, you'll be encouraged to embrace the deeper meaning of mindfulness and establish your own daily practice.

In the meantime, let's get started by exploring what it really means to get one second ahead.

CHAPTER 1

Mastering Your Mind—First Steps

Jacob was a senior manager in a European financial services company. Like most of his counterparts, he was always "on"—connected to the office in one way or another, all day, every day. Day in, day out, he dealt with a steady stream of e-mails and an overloaded calendar of meetings. When he did have a free moment, he would often be interrupted by someone phoning with yet another urgent matter that needed his immediate attention.

When I first met Jacob, he told me that he didn't feel in control of his life. He felt like he was always trying to catch up, always overloaded with external forces—people and tasks—dictating his day-to-day reality. He felt he was living on autopilot without a clear sense of purpose and direction.

Sound familiar?

Like many of us, Jacob longed for a greater sense of control. A friend of his had recently been to one of my workshops and suggested Jacob give me a call. In our first meeting, he committed to undertake a four-month program based on the tools, techniques, and strategies presented in this book. During that time, we met for ten one-hour sessions and he dedicated ten minutes a day to mindfulness training. Though it was specifically designed as a convenient, user-friendly program, it was still a significant investment of time considering his already busy work schedule.

After the four months had gone by, I asked Jacob what he'd gained from the program.

His answer: "One second."

At first, his response took me by surprise. Four months of effort and daily training to gain only one second? That seemed like a meager return.

But then he explained, "Previously, when something happened, I reacted automatically. Every time an e-mail came in, I read it. Every time I received a text, I answered it. Whenever a thought or emotion popped into my head, I paid attention to it and allowed it to take my focus away from what I was doing. I was a victim of my own automatic reactions. The four months of training have given me a one-second mental gap between what happens and my own response. It feels like I'm one second ahead, so that I can choose my response rather than being a victim of my automatic reactions. I can't always control what happens in life, but I've developed the freedom to choose my response to it."

Jacob's story clearly describes what millions of busy people experience every day.

But one second? What can change in one second?

Everything.

One second is the difference between catching the train or being late for work. It's the difference between making a yellow light or running a red. It's the difference between a close call or a catastrophe.

In the Olympics, one second separates winning gold and being immortalized from coming in last and being forgotten.

In our low-latency world, speed is a factor in any competition—sports, politics, and especially business. This is more true now than ever before. With today's high-frequency trading, millions of dollars can change hands in a millisecond. That's one-tenth the time it takes to blink. As the speed of business approaches the speed of light, one second is the difference between performance and *high* performance.

For Jacob, one second gave him the freedom to control his thoughts, his actions, and, more profoundly, his life.

This chapter aims to jump-start your transformation toward gaining that one-second advantage in your own life. Together, we'll examine our natural cognitive tendencies, the effect these tendencies have on productivity, and some simple—but very powerful—rules for increasing mental effectiveness.

Who Is in Control?

Life is about results. Results come from our actions. Our actions come from the choices we make. Our choices come from the thoughts we think (see Figure 1.1).

Our thoughts are the foundation for everything we want to achieve in life. Thus, our ability to manage our mind becomes critically important. We are best able to manage our thoughts when our mind is clear, calm, and focused. This is true in all aspects of life, but especially true in the workplace.

According to scientists, however, on average our mind is wandering almost half our waking hours.[1] We are constantly thinking about events that happened in the past, or might happen in the future, rather than attending to what's happening right now. This limits our ability to achieve meaningful results.

Does this apply to you? Here's a quick test to find out.

1. Set a timer for 45 seconds.
2. Focus your attention on one thought—an e-mail, a meeting, or something else.
3. Focus your full attention on this one thing and nothing else.
4. Do not pay attention to any other thoughts or sounds until the time is over.

Were you able to maintain focus on one thing? If you are like most people, you likely experienced that, during those brief 45 seconds, your mind wandered off to a variety of thoughts. Don't worry—you're perfectly normal.

Figure 1.1   Results come from your mind.

If you can relate to this experience, then you probably recognize that sometimes—or possibly often—your mind has a mind of its own. In other words, it can be difficult to control your mind and what you pay attention to. But if it's true that our thoughts shape our future, and we are really not in control of our thoughts, it raises an important question: Who's making the decisions in our lives?

For many of us, this question is becoming tougher to answer. The natural tendency for our mind to wander has worsened over the past few decades. Before the advent of the desktop computer, smartphones, and the Internet, it was easier for people to give their full attention to each task at hand. But within a relatively short span of time, we've gone from handling a typewriter and a telephone to juggling e-mails, texts, tweets, spreadsheets, reports, deadlines, and much more—all at the same time. We have mountains of evidence, as well as stacks of reports, articles, and books, outlining the detrimental effect that our recent digital immersion has had on focus and productivity.

Welcome to the Attention Economy

Work life has changed radically over the past few decades. We used to have working conditions where our attention could more easily focus on the task at hand. We are now experiencing distractions and information overload all the time. Our cell phones, tablets, e-mails, texts, and the like place constant demands on our attention. According to the former director of the Accenture Institute of Strategic Change, Tom Davenport, "Understanding and managing attention is now the single most important determinant of business success."[2]

We are living in an "attention economy" where the ability to manage our attention and the quality of our attention is key to our success. But in the digital age, where our ability to pay attention at will is under siege, we have a problem.

How big is this problem? Researchers studying the mind's natural tendency to wander calculated that on average our mind wanders 46.9 percent of the time.[3] In other words, while we are at work, 53.1 percent of the time our mind is on task. The rest of the time it is off task. From a human resource perspective, there is a lot of potential to be developed here. Even just a small increase in "on-task" time could have a significant improvement in many aspects of work, including productivity, customer service, safety, teamwork, and anything else that would benefit from more focused attention.

Attention is indeed a new variable of performance in business. Traditionally, business productivity has been enhanced through time management, goal setting, prioritization skills, and general qualifications. Attention, in the digital age, is becoming a new enabler of business performance. Welcome to the attention economy.

Researchers have found that the brain has a default way of reacting to the relentless flow of distractions in the digital age: it tries to attend to it all at the same time. It defaults to multitasking. And who wouldn't love to be able to get more accomplished by doing multiple tasks at the same time? Some companies even include "good at multitasking" as a requirement in job descriptions. But when we try to multitask, the research shows, we take more time, make more mistakes, and use up more mental energy.

Multitasking Is a Myth

Most of us carry around the powerful illusion that we can pay attention to more than one thing at a time. We think we can drive a car while talking on the phone, participate in a meeting while checking e-mails, or engage in a conversation while writing a text message. To be clear, we can do many activities without paying attention, that is, without conscious thought. For example, we can walk and talk at the same time. Experienced drivers can handle many of the elements of driving, such as changing gears and turning the wheel, on autopilot.

But from a neurological perspective, we're not capable of focusing attention on two things at the same time. When we think we are multitasking, what we are doing in reality is *shift-tasking*: shifting attention rapidly between two or more things. For example, when talking on the phone while driving, for a second, we're aware of traffic, and then the next second, of the phone. Sometimes we switch so quickly between tasks we have the illusion we're paying attention to both at the same time, but in actuality, we aren't.

The Noncomputational Brain

The term "multitasking" comes from the computer industry and describes a computer's ability to process several different data sets in parallel. Computers today have no trouble running an Excel spreadsheet, playing a video, sending and receiving e-mails, and scanning for viruses all at the same time. This highlights a big difference between a computer and a human: a computer has several processors, all operating at the same time, while a human has only one brain and a singular attention.

When we have many things we have to get done, many of us try to be efficient and effective by doing more than one thing at a time. The reality is, as amazing and powerful as our brains are, we're not capable of focusing our attention on two things at the same time.

In the context of multitasking at work, researchers have found that "multitaskers are masters of everything that is irrelevant, they let themselves be distracted by anything."[4] Perhaps you've experienced losing track of what you are doing even when you have a simple task and clear intentions. For example, say you want to send your mother a gift for her birthday, so you go online to search for something she would like. While searching for books in Amazon, you find a couple books to add to your own wish list. Then you notice a link in one of the book's comments to an article that looks interesting. You hit that link and start reading, and find a link to a cool video on YouTube. An hour later, you catch yourself still watching videos and have completely lost track of what you started out to do.

Studies have shown that multitasking lowers people's job satisfaction, damages personal relationships, adversely affects memory, and negatively impacts health.[5] Many of these studies have demonstrated that multitasking reduces effectiveness because it takes longer to complete tasks and leads to more mistakes. This is because when we switch our focus from one task to another, it takes time to make the shift. Depending on the complexity of the new task, that can take anywhere from a few seconds to several minutes. This phenomenon is called *shift-time*. Shift-time saps our mental energy and taxes our productivity.

In addition, researchers from Harvard Business School discovered that multitasking hinders creativity.[6] They assessed 9,000 employees who were working on projects that required creative and innovative thinking. They found a notable drop in creative thinking among employees who multitasked and an increase in creativity among employees who focused on one task at a time.

In summary, when we multitask, we're less effective, make more mistakes, and have less focus and creativity. But if multitasking is so bad, why do so many of us continue to do it?

Because it's addictive. Shifting rapidly back and forth between tasks often feels exciting, even though it's physically draining and stressful.[7] In a separate study, researchers at Harvard University discovered that multitasking provides a "dopamine injection" to the brain.[8] Dopamine is a naturally produced neurotransmitter in the brain that is directly linked to addiction. When released in the brain, it provides a sense of enjoyment and gratification. Because of this instant gratification, the brain is constantly looking for a new dopamine kick—and quick, easily achieved tasks like e-mail do the trick. As it turns out, multitasking actually trains the brain to welcome distraction and all the inefficiencies it creates.

But there is a way to break the habit.

The Well-Trained Mind

Mindfulness is about you. It's about overcoming the multitasking trap, and entering the attention economy being one second ahead of your wandering mind and external distractions. It's about being the best version of yourself every day. It's about generating greater mental effectiveness so that you can reach your full potential, both on a professional *and* a personal level. Effectiveness in this context is the ability to achieve your goals, objectives, and wishes in life.

Mindfulness training has been developed over thousands of years. In recent decades it has spread widely in the West, taking form through different interpretations and applications. In our work, we keep the definition of mindfulness close to its ancient description: a mind in balance, which sees reality clearly and values ethics. A balanced mind is relaxed, focused, and clear. A mind that sees clearly views, reality as ever changing, as mere potential, and knows the difference between genuine happiness and fleeting pleasure. Valuing ethics means continually discerning what's wholesome and constructive and what is not.

Ancient Wisdom, Modern Work

In an attention economy, mindfulness is about learning to master your attention. When you learn to master your attention, you learn to master your thoughts. You learn to hold your focus on what you choose, whether it's this page, an e-mail, a meeting, your spouse, or your children. In other words, you train yourself to be more present in the here and now.

Over the years, working with thousands of people around the globe, I've seen formal mindfulness training help individuals become calmer and clearer minded. With a calmer and clearer mind, people are able to greatly enhance performance, effectiveness, collaboration, and gain a clearer perspective on life and the choices they make.

But don't take my word for it. Since the first controlled experiments with mindfulness, the scientific world has discovered the wide-ranging benefits of mindfulness training. Mindfulness has a positive impact on our physiology, mental processes, and work performance. At the physiological level, researchers have demonstrated that mindfulness training can result in a stronger immune system,[9] lower blood pressure,[10] and a lower heart rate.[11] People sleep better[12] and feel less stressed.[13]

Mindfulness training increases the density of grey cells in our cerebral cortex, the part of the brain that thinks rationally and solves problems.[14] Cognitive function improves, resulting in better memory,[15] increased concentration,[16] reduced cognitive rigidity,[17] and faster reaction times.[18] Not surprisingly, people who practice mindfulness techniques report an overall increase in quality of life.[19]

These results are clearly beneficial in a corporate context, where they can be realized in a relatively short period of time. For example, a researcher from Singapore Management University evaluated the effectiveness of our corporate mindfulness programs at Carlsberg, a global consumer goods giant, and If Insurance, a large European insurance company. He found significant improvements in focus, awareness, memory, job performance, and overall job satisfaction after only nine weeks of training. Employees also reported reduced stress and improved perceptions of work-life balance.[20] Other researchers have found similar benefits from mindfulness training in corporate contexts, including:

- Increased creativity and innovation;[21]
- improved employer-employee relations;[22]
- reduced absenteeism due to illness;[23] and
- improved ethical decision-making.[24]

Mindfulness training is ultimately a tool for developing a highly functional and effective mind. Fortunately for all of us, groundbreaking research over the past three decades has demonstrated that attention, like many other brain functions, can be trained.

The Adaptive Brain

Training our brain is possible because of what's scientifically termed *neuroplasticity*. In short, neuroplasticity describes the structural flexibility of our brains, including the ability to create new neural pathways through practice and repetition. Neuroscientists explain it with the simple saying, "neurons that fire together, wire together."

Research shows that we demonstrate pronounced neuroplasticity throughout our adult lives. This type of neural modification occurs through learning a new skill, whether it's juggling, playing golf, plucking a banjo—or training our attention by practicing mindfulness. Anything we do becomes easier to do again, because our brains create new and stronger neural connections every time we do it. For all of us, this should be good news: we're not limited or defined by the faculties and aptitudes we've already developed. Instead, we can keep learning and growing and effectively rewiring our brain throughout our entire lives. And we can overcome some of the detrimental attentional consequences of modern work life.

This leads us to the basis of mindfulness training.

The Foundation of Mindfulness

The central characteristics of mindfulness are *sharp focus* and *open awareness*. Sharp focus is the ability to concentrate single-pointedly on any object of choice for a long as you want with minimal effort. Training sharp focus provides the benefit of being fully present with other people or tasks. Open awareness is the ability to see clearly what is happening in your mind and make wise choices about where to focus your attention. Through training open awareness, you gain clarity. The clutter from the outer world and from your own mind is reduced. As you become more insightful, even the most difficult problems appear less complex and become easier to handle. Optimal effectiveness is achieved when people are simultaneously sharply focused and openly aware. This is the essence of being mindful and the goal you can work toward throughout this book.

Of course, gaining this level of insight and a trained mind takes time, effort, and deliberate practice. As you progress through this book, my hope is you begin applying mindfulness to all aspects of your life, whether at work or at home. But for now, let's focus on the small steps you can take to immediately improve your performance and your results in the workplace. This begins by understanding focus and awareness in action, or, what we call, the two rules for mental effectiveness.

Two Rules of Mental Effectiveness

There are two basic rules that help you manage your focus and awareness in all activities to ensure greater effectiveness, less/stress, better job satisfaction, and an improved overall sense of well-being. These rules also help to reduce your brain's tendency to multitask. These two rules are based on the foundational trainings in mindfulness described in Chapters 2 and 3.

Rule #1: Focus on What You Choose

Staying focused on the object of your choice is the first rule of mental effectiveness. A focused mind helps you be more effective, productive, and at ease while doing your work. A focused mind does not multitask: instead, it's fully present on the person or task at hand.

To help bring this rule to life, consider the following scenario. On Monday morning, you arrive at work and are handed a task that needs to be finished in 30 minutes. To meet the deadline, you make this task the object of your focus. A coworker next to you starts talking on the telephone. Normally, your attention would wander away to your neighbor's conversation. Instead, you follow Rule #1 and stay focused on the task. You do this by recognizing that your neighbor's conversation is a distraction. Now you can make a choice. You can either choose to focus on the distraction or continue to maintain full focus on the task at hand.

Then an e-mail alert pops up. It attracts your attention. You feel a strong desire to see who sent the e-mail. But instead, you make a conscious choice to continue attending to the task at hand. So you let go of the new distraction and stay on task. You continue to make these types of conscious decisions throughout the half hour, until you've finished the task.

Focusing on what you choose depends on recognizing that the overwhelming majority of distractions are irrelevant and can be set aside in the moment. Almost all distractions should be let go. The awareness component of mindfulness training shows you that most of your thoughts are mental clutter. Your surroundings are also full of things you don't need to pay attention to in the moment. By consciously choosing where to focus your attention, you avoid becoming a victim of distraction. As simple as it sounds, Rule #1 is a powerful way to increase productivity and effectiveness.

Of course, some distractions do require our immediate attention. For example, let's imagine you're maintaining sharp focus on your task, and your boss walks up to your desk. She's agitated and says the company is about to lose its biggest account. She needs you in her office, "Now." But because of Rule #1, you ignore her and continue working on your task.

Would that be effective? No, of course not. And it might even get you fired.

Helpfulness, availability, and open communication are critical for organizational success. If we all focused solely on the tasks at hand, collaboration and creativity would suffer. So, while Rule #1 works most of the time, it isn't enough. We need a second rule.

Rule #2: Choose Your Distractions Mindfully

Rule #2 ensures you work in a focused way while remaining open to your surroundings and recognizing when you should change focus.

Let's look at the previous scenario again in light of Rule #2. When your coworker started talking on the telephone or the e-mail alert popped up, you did the right thing by letting go of these distractions. You needed to make a different choice, however, when your boss came up to your desk.

Rule #2 invites us to make a subtle evaluation of every distraction. Should I deal with this distraction now or let it go? If you want to keep your job, the correct response to your boss would be to give her your full attention.

This doesn't mean you keep working on the task and shift your attention back and forth between your boss and your task. That would be multitasking, and we already know that doesn't work. Instead, Rule #2 requires consciously choosing to let go of the task you were working on and focusing your full attention on your boss. Rule #1 becomes re-engaged at this point.

When you apply both rules, you have three options for responding to any distraction:

1. You can choose not to deal with the distraction and let it go completely. Then return to your task with full focus.
2. You can tell the distraction (external or internal) that you will deal with it at a specific time in the future. Then return to your task with full focus.
3. You can choose to fully turn your attention to the distraction and make it the new object of your focus. Your previous task is set aside to be dealt with at a specific time in the future.

The reality for most of us is that we need to manage many different tasks, projects, or people within limited time frames. While trying to hold them all center stage in your mind doesn't work, mindfully shifting between tasks, projects, or people does. To explore this further, let's place the two rules within a matrix that maps different levels of mental effectiveness in the context of work.

Mindfulness Applied

When applying both rules for mental effectiveness, you focus on what you're doing and you remain aware of which distractions to pay attention to and which ones to let go. Understandably, though, we often find ourselves in situations in which we apply one rule but not the other. To better understand how the two rules work together, see Figure 1.2.

As the first quadrant shows, when you are focused but on autopilot, your state of mind can be described as being in "flow." Some people prefer to be in this state, especially when they're tackling routine tasks or physical work. Flow is characterized by some degree of absorption and therefore lacking awareness of external distractions. This can pose a problem even during routine work, because you may neglect sensory signals of important events around you or physiological signals indicating you need rest, movement, or food. We need awareness to pick up on relevant distractions—like our boss coming into our office—or signals

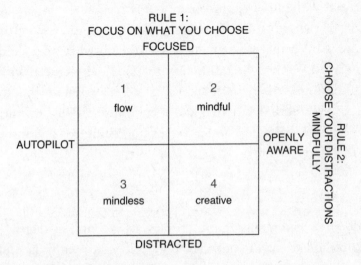

Figure 1.2 The Matrix of Mental Effectiveness.

from our body. Although many things can be done on autopilot, most of the time it is beneficial to remain aware of our surroundings.

In the fourth quadrant, you're aware but easily distracted. There can be benefits to loosening focus and allowing random thoughts to bubble up. Some people find that they come up with more creative ideas in this quadrant. But if your mind is too distracted, you'll have difficulty retaining any good ideas. Good ideas only become innovative solutions when you have the focus to retain and execute them.

In the third quadrant, you're neither focused nor aware. Some people see this quadrant as the most relaxing. Taking a closer look, though, you may find that is not the case. Next time you find yourself daydreaming on distracted autopilot, check in with your experience: are you truly relaxed? With a bit of training you will see that a focused mind is much more relaxed than a distracted mind. Further, it's obviously not a very useful state of mind in a work context. Often, when I explain the matrix to a group, people say they want to be in the third quadrant when they face something unpleasant like going to the dentist. They say they'd rather be numb to the experience, or unaware and distracted. But based on my own experience, even in painful situations there's a benefit to maintaining a focused and aware mind.

In the second quadrant—defined as "mindful"—we have the greatest mental bandwidth to complete tasks and the highest quality of interactions with our environment and other people. Representing the junction of the two rules of mental effectiveness, the second quadrant equates to being present with ourselves and what we're doing. It helps us when we encounter difficult situations and is crucial when we want to optimize our performance at work. It's a state of mind that is one second ahead of external and mental distractions. It's the best response to the digital age and a way of improving your performance in an attention economy.

Perpetual Obstacles

This doesn't mean attaining mindfulness is as simple as merely identifying the quadrant of your choice. We all consistently face obstacles to maintaining focus and awareness. For most people, the biggest challenge is their own mind. If you're used to multitasking, you'll be tempted again and again to try to do more than one thing at a time. Every time you catch yourself, pause and then choose to maintain focus on one thing. After a while, you'll create new neural connections and form new habits.

The other big challenge many people encounter is their coworkers, work culture, and office layout, especially in open-office environments. Many organizations operate with implicit assumptions around availability and urgency. Although people being available and able to respond to urgent tasks is fundamental to business success, it needs to be balanced with a recognition of how people can maximize mental performance through applying the two rules of mental effectiveness. By maintaining an appropriate level of awareness, you can find this balance and stay sensitive to situations that necessitate a shift in focus.

A New Way of Working

Simply put, the way many of us are working is *not* working.

We need another approach.

Combining the two rules of mental effectiveness—focus on what you choose and choose your distractions mindfully—results in a new way of working that can truly optimize individual performance. The key elements of the two rules are straightforward: give full conscious attention to whatever you're doing at the moment. When you write an e-mail, give it your full attention. When you're with other people, be fully present with them. Don't try to do two cognitive tasks at the same time. Your attention will become fragmented and the important things will suffer.

The advantages to this approach are significant, including greater productivity, improved performance, and less stress. Maintaining focus and choosing your distractions wisely allows you to stay one second ahead of your own reactions, to actively choose your response to events in your inner and outer worlds instead of reacting on autopilot. Simple, yet deeply insightful, these two rules help strip away the noise and disruptions that can clutter your mind and sidetrack you on the way to attaining your goals.

In the remainder of Part I of the book, I'll examine how you can apply what you've learned in this chapter to crucial elements of your work life. Divided into succinct, self-contained modules, the following pages provide techniques that improve performance, enhance creativity, increase energy, and bolster resilience.

As you immerse yourself in the coming techniques of this book, I encourage you to do so in a mindful way. From time to time, take a short pause, focusing on your breath for a moment. As you do so, check the quality of your mind: which quadrant is it in? If you find yourself in anything else than the second quadrant, stay with your breath for a few minutes and allow your attention to center and calm down. Then continue reading.

TECHNIQUE #1

E-mails

In 1971, Ray Tomlinson, a computer engineer in Massachusetts, knocked on his top row of keys, transmitting "QWERTYUIOP" from his computer to another computer sitting in the same room. And just like that, e-mail was born.

Since then, e-mail has spread quickly. Recent studies show the average person sends and receives around 100 e-mails a day.[1]

Regardless of your job, your location, or your industry, e-mail probably takes up a significant portion of your time at work—while not always producing the best results. This technique, I offer seven simple ways mindfulness can make you more efficient and effective at using e-mail, as well as other electronic forms of communication like texting, office messaging systems, and the like.

Guideline #1: Avoid E-mail Addiction

How often do you check your e-mail? A few times a day? Hourly? Every time that gadget in your pocket buzzes or lights up? Can you honestly go without checking your e-mail for any significant stretch of time?

If not, you're not alone. One report shows 60 percent of Americans check their e-mail on vacation, and 25 percent become restless and unwell after just three days without access to e-mail.[2] In fact, doctors have estimated 11 million Americans suffer from "e-mail addiction."[3]

If you think this sounds crazy, think again.

E-mail dependency is principally the same as any other type of dependency. When you receive a grateful message from a client, praise from your boss, an interesting article, or a funny joke, your brain releases dopamine—a neurotransmitter that makes you feel good. Craving that lift from a nice or funny e-mail creates a tendency to check your e-mail more and more often.

Mindfulness training puts you better in tune with your thoughts, feelings, and cravings. When you get the urge to check your e-mail for its own sake, observe it. Before you automatically succumb to that urge, pause. Take just one second. And in that second, you'll come to see there's nothing necessarily automatic about your responses to stimuli.

You have a choice.

Sometimes, one second of mindful contemplation is all it takes to resist an automatic impulse. There are a number of things you can do to increase your chances of success in mitigating or avoiding e-mail addiction. The first is to eliminate all notifications.

Guideline #2: Kill All Notifications

Having your e-mail always on, even if only in the background, can create a lot of unnecessary "noise" both in the lives of individuals and within functioning organizations. One of the simplest ways to create more time and improve mental focus is to eliminate unnecessary noise. When it comes to e-mail, you can do yourself a favor by switching off your e-mail notifications, pop-up windows, alarms, and ring tones. Doing so will keep your time between designated e-mail sessions clear for other, more important work.

Over the next couple of days, pay attention to what happens to your focus, your productivity, and your well-being each time you're distracted by an e-mail notification. Then try working for a couple days with the notifications switched off. After that, you can make an informed decision about what works best for you.

A lot of the time, getting a new e-mail pulls our focus away from the job at hand, forcing us to shift from task to task. The next guideline for mindful e-mailing is to stop that shifting before it starts.

Guideline #3: Mind Your Switch Time

Addicted or not, many people leave their e-mail open all day long. It helps them feel like they're perpetually productive and constantly up to date. Always online, they often answer e-mails shortly after receiving them. That might be helpful if someone needs an immediate response, but it can also cause its own problems.

If you allow your focus to shift every time a new e-mail arrives, you're wasting time. It takes your brain several seconds to concentrate on a new e-mail, and then the same time again to return your focus to your previous work—or perhaps even longer, if you've lost your place or your train of thought. Besides taking up time, shifting back and forth between tasks uses up a lot of energy, making you less effective overall.

To most effectively minimize your switch time, remember the two rules of mental effectiveness outlined in Chapter 1: *Focus on what you choose* and *choose your distractions mindfully.* If you allow every new e-mail that hits your inbox to distract you, you're not choosing your distractions mindfully.

Consider for a moment what impact checking e-mails has in terms of your mental effectiveness. For most people, it brings them down toward the distracted and autopilot end of The Matrix of Mental Effectiveness (see Figure T1.1).

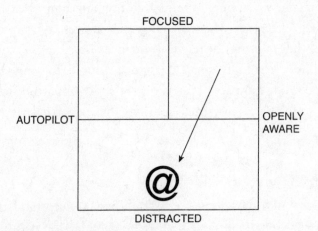

Figure T1.1 E-mails in the Matrix.

Beyond turning off your notifications and minding your switch time, you can structure your e-mailing in a way that ensures the most effective use of your hours in the office or on the job.

Guideline #4: Never First Thing in the Morning

In the first half of the morning, the brain is generally most alert, most focused, and most creative. Many people open their e-mail first thing in the morning, even though that might not be the best use of that period of exceptional focus and creativity.

Opening your e-mail first thing in the morning immediately draws you into an onslaught of short-term problems. As your brain adapts to the pace of e-mail, your early morning creative energy dissipates. Choosing e-mail as your first task of the day can be a wasted opportunity to use your mind at its highest potential. Instead, try waiting at least half an hour to an hour after you get to work before checking your inbox.

Whenever you ultimately decide to schedule your e-mail sessions, be sure to put these sessions on your calendar as fixed activities, with the rest of your activities planned around them.

Guideline #5: Secure Focus Time

If you're checking and responding to e-mails all day, you're not fully focused on your work, on your e-mails, or on anything else. Instead of shifting your attention whenever an e-mail arrives, allocate only certain, fixed times during the day to fully focus on e-mail.

Sometimes, seemingly small changes to our daily work lives can have an enormous impact. This is one of those opportunities. When securing your own focus time, consider these questions: how often, how long, and when?

How Often to Check E-mail

In the course of a day, how often should you concentrate on e-mail? The answer depends on your own temperament, the nature of your work, and the culture in your organization. Whatever you do, don't check your e-mail on autopilot. Create separation between yourself and your inbox; give yourself time to focus specifically on other things. Then give yourself time to focus specifically on e-mail. Both your overall job performance and your resulting e-mails will be better for it.

How Long to Focus on E-mail

How long should your e-mail sessions last? That depends on the volume of e-mails you receive and send every day. Take the total time you anticipate spending on e-mail and divide that by the number of e-mail sessions you anticipate in a day (likely two or three). That should give you a starting point for how much time to allocate for each e-mail session. If you're focused and efficient, you'll often find you don't end up using all of the allocated time. This time can then be repurposed for other activities or tasks in the office.

When to Schedule E-mail Sessions

When should you deal with your e-mail? This depends on your general daily program and your organization's culture. One e-mail session in the morning (again, not first thing) and one again in the afternoon is ideal. If three are necessary, consider adding a short session just before or after lunch.

Of course, there's more to mindful e-mail than structuring your time effectively. It's also important to consider the content and tone of your messages—the "stuff" of e-mail. Start by avoiding bad vibes in the e-mail you send to others.

Guideline #6: Avoid Bad Vibes

When the mind receives too little information about a sender's intentions, it composes its own story. Individuals are often convinced a self-created story is true. To make matters worse, the mind has a tendency to emphasize negative stories over positive ones. In other words, we tend to assume the worst. But why?

In their book *Louder Than Words...Nonverbal Communication*, Mele Koneya and Alton Barbour suggest that one of the fundamental

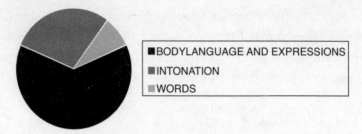

Figure T1.2   Communication channels.

reasons we struggle with effective electronic communication is simply that words are not the primary way we internalize messages.[4] In fact, research has shown that 60 percent of communication is understood through body language, and another 33 percent through tone of voice. That leaves only 7 percent for the actual words (see Figure T1.2).

Since e-mail only uses 7 percent of your communication potential, there's an enormously high probability for misunderstanding. In this sense, autopilot can be your worst enemy. Improving your awareness can make you far less likely to create misunderstanding, worry, and conflict.

Three questions can help you avoid bad vibes and be more mindful before you hit "send":

1. *Should this e-mail be sent at all? And should all these people be copied?* E-mail is widely overused. Make sure you're not just adding to the chatter. Make sure your e-mail really needs to be sent. It's okay to delete an e-mail if it really isn't that important.
2. *Does the e-mail contain the information needed for it to be understood correctly?* We've all sent or received a message without an attachment or other key detail. Oversights like these can cause multiple messages to go back and forth, all with similar questions. Make sure you aren't wasting valuable time—yours or anyone else's.
3. *How will the recipient perceive this e-mail?* Put yourself in the recipient's shoes. How can you phrase this note to best avoid negative speculation in the recipient's mind? Taking just one second to think about how your e-mail will be perceived can be

the difference between clear communication and an unfortunate misunderstanding. One thing is certain: saying "thanks" and "sorry" are always good ideas.

Of course, we've all sent a note or two we wish we hadn't. Through mindfulness, you get yourself one second ahead of that hasty response or ill-conceived note. And this takes us to the next guideline: avoid emotional e-mailing.

Guideline #7: Avoid Emotional E-mailing

When it comes to e-mail, there's a much wider variety of potential interpretations compared to communicating in person. Avoiding emotional e-mailing means being aware of your own thought patterns: it means being aware of the stories your mind creates before you end up believing them or making them worse.

While most e-mails are positive or neutral, there are always exceptions. Before you start reading e-mails, take a few moments to relax. When you come across an e-mail that generates negative reactions, stop. *Do not* give in to the impulse to answer immediately. Let me repeat that: do not give in to impulse to answer immediately. Instead, start by thinking calmly about how the e-mail makes you feel: defensive? angry? sad? Then praise yourself for being aware of your own reactions to the e-mail. Remember the limitations of the medium; it's only 7 percent of communication.

Although it can be tempting to vent your frustrations, an impulsive answer can easily cause more harm than good. Have the courage to tolerate your discomfort. Face the impulse head-on. But do not give in to it.

Take the time to think about what kind of response will have the most beneficial outcome, both for you and the sender. Maybe the best response isn't an e-mail at all, but a quick call to air out an issue or clear up any misunderstanding. This may allow you to let go of the situation completely instead of ruminating about it.

When it comes to mindful e-mail, following these seven simple guidelines can save a lot of time, as well as reduce stress and increase mental effectiveness. The next technique presents ways to bring more mindfulness into meetings.

Tips and Reflections for Mindful E-mailing

- Take a moment to reflect on your use of e-mail and your relationship with your inbox—is e-mail a source of distraction for you?
- Consider when and how you use e-mail, including setting clear guidelines on when you use it and how applying mindfulness to sending and receiving e-mails could be of benefit.
- To enhance effectiveness and increase mental space, engage your colleagues in a discussion on your e-mail culture.

TECHNIQUE #2

Meetings

The way many organizations conduct meetings leaves much to be desired. In fact, more often than not, people find meetings to be a waste of time. A few different studies have shown that managers and executives feel somewhere between 25 percent and 50 percent of time spent in meetings to be wasted.[1]

And it gets worse.

One study by American Online and Salary.com found the average American worker only *actually works three days per week*.[2] Three days? It sure doesn't feel that way. But the other two days, the study argues, are taken up by unproductive activities like inefficient or unnecessary meetings.

Meetings are supposed to allow us to benefit from collective wisdom and experience, ideally allowing us to accomplish things we couldn't otherwise do on our own. When people are not fully present in meetings, however, we don't get the best out of each other. We don't make use of our creative potential. And quite often, we waste a lot of time.

This technique looks at ways we can use mindfulness as an effective tool to get the most out of meetings in the shortest time possible.

Three Phases of Mindful Meetings

To implement mindful meetings, start by considering one simple question: are your meetings for your benefit and the benefit of others? If the answer is "yes," then your primary concern should be making meetings more effective for yourself and for others. Thinking of meetings in three phases—preparation, the meeting itself, and the end—can help you optimize your time in meetings and ensure a better outcome for everyone involved.

Mental Preparation

It's been said that a good start is half of getting wherever you want to go. This is particularly true for meetings.

A good start to a meeting means your mind is clear, having let go of whatever you were talking about or working on before the meeting. It also requires shifting your focus onto three things: the people you're with, the meeting agenda, and yourself.

As important as mental preparation is, it usually takes less than a minute. It can be done individually or as a group. If you do it alone, it's easy and flexible.

Here's what to do: before you enter the meeting room, direct your full attention to your breath, letting each and every distraction pass like waves crashing on a beach. In a single minute, you can bring yourself into the present moment and be ready for what comes next. Wherever you choose to prepare—at your desk, on the way to the meeting, or in the meeting room before others arrive—the crucial part is to stay focused on your breathing, as you let go of internal and external distractions.

While doing your own mental preparation can be beneficial, preparing as a group can help improve the mental effectiveness of everyone in attendance. You don't even need to call it mindfulness. Before you introduce an agenda, simply invite meeting participants to take a brief mental break, to relax, settle their mind, and become present in the room. Sitting in a room silently for a few moments can create a strong feeling of togetherness and unity.

Consider Mette, People Group Director at a global consumer beverages company. From morning to evening, her days are filled with meetings. For her, and many of her staff, introducing mental preparation into their regular routine for meetings led to a significant boost in terms of overall effectiveness. In speaking with her about her experience, she shared, "Our buildings are a long way apart from each other, which gives us plenty of time to prepare ourselves mentally for meetings. In addition, we often have one minute of silence together before starting the meeting. By applying these simple strategies to our meetings, we find meetings take less time and are a lot more enjoyable, even when we are addressing challenging topics. Everything is better and easier when we are present with each other."

For Mette and her staff, it didn't take major changes to their routine to become more present and enjoy more effective meetings. Simply using transition time and a minute at the start of each meeting for mental preparation transformed their meeting culture, as well as their overall effectiveness as a team.

Try it. Purposeful mental preparation really is a great way to focus the mind and clear away the mental clutter before diving into the content of the actual meeting.

The Actual Meeting

A clear purpose, a defined agenda, agreeing on timing, managing tangents, and adhering to timelines are all solid guidelines for conducting effective meetings. Even with all of these standards in place, a meeting is only effective if everyone is paying attention. If participants have their laptops open or phones in hand, the collective mental capacity that should be the hallmark of successful meetings simply isn't there.

If someone chooses to respond to a text message, that person has in effect left the meeting. Not only is the person who's answering texts not fully present in the meeting, but he or she is also distracting everyone else. Every time an individual checks e-mail or shoots off a text, other people think about checking their phones—or they simply become irritated by the person who's not paying attention. Then that same person may ask a question that's already been answered, detracting further from the flow of the meeting and creating even greater frustration.

We've all experienced some version of this scenario: we've all seen how energy and productivity can start to decline as people become more and more distracted, increasingly frustrated, or visibly annoyed. Distracted meetings take longer. They're less effective. And, frankly, they're unpleasant experiences.

In meetings, presence forms the foundation for effectiveness. When we're present with other people, we get the most out of our time together. Therefore, the fundamental rule for a mindful meeting is: be completely present with those you are together with for as long as you are together.

Every meeting you're in, you have the opportunity to make the people you're with the anchor of your attention. To do so, focus your attention on the person who is speaking. Sometimes it can be a challenge to be fully present, especially when meetings are long or cover topics that aren't directly relevant to your work. With practice, it gets easier. And after some time, it becomes your default mode.

Certainly, there are times when computers and phones are important during a meeting. But before turning them on, ensure their use is tied to helping enhance the meeting instead of simply acting as a convenient distraction. Similarly, when your phone buzzes, pause for a second. Think about your priorities and goals. Think about the impact being less present will have on the rest of the meeting. Odds are, the message or text can wait.

These same guidelines apply to virtual meetings, conference calls, and other forms of remote meetings. Since you're not face to face with people, it can be especially challenging to maintain focus. And while it would be great to say that mindfulness training can magically make all your meetings 100 percent effective, it's just not that easy. It's important to recognize that you have choices. If you're on a conference call and decide to quietly finish an e-mail, you're at risk of missing something important and potentially decreasing the meeting's effectiveness for everyone.

In this way, mindfulness is a tremendous help. It can help you improve focus during the meeting, be more aware of any distractions, and develop the clarity necessary to make good, in-the-moment decisions.

Ending the Meeting

Concluding meetings at the right time and in the right way can be an art. It's important to be mindful of ending meetings on time so that everyone can move on to their next activity. As a meeting up wraps, be sure any "action items," "follow-ups," or "next steps" are clearly documented and assigned.

Fitting in some time at the end of a meeting to practice mindfulness can also be of benefit in terms of softening a hard stop. Taking just a few minutes can help further clear the mind and increase relaxation, focus, and clarity for upcoming activities.

In fact, some companies have begun letting meetings finish a few minutes early, giving participants the opportunity to settle and clear their minds before their next activity. Also, if the meeting finishes at an appropriate time, there's less of a rush. This means you have the opportunity to look coworkers in the eye and thank them for their time and attention. When a meeting is concluded with gratitude and appreciation, people are more willing to meet again and a positive pattern for meetings develops.

Life's Most Important Meetings

The most important meetings in life don't take place in boardrooms or conference rooms. In fact, they're not work related at all. Life's most important "meetings" are the ones you share with your partner, your children, other family members, and your friends. These are the moments in which your full attention and presence are even more important and most precious.

When you look back on your life, will you ever think about the meetings you had at work? Not likely. Odds are, you'll look back at the time you spent with the people you care most about. If it's important to be present anywhere, it's important to be present with your family and friends. As Brian Dyson, the former CEO of Coca-Cola, said as part of a commencement speech at a major American university:

Imagine life as a game where you're juggling five balls in the air. The five balls are work, family, health, friends, and happiness. You'll soon find out that your work is a rubber ball; if you drop it, it bounces back into your hands. But the other four balls are made of glass. If you drop any of them, they'll be forever damaged, broken, or completely destroyed. They'll never be the same again. So work effectively when you're at work and go home on time. Give the necessary time to your family and your friends and look after yourself. A value only has value if it is valued.[3]

Consider the results, benefits, and payoffs in your life if more mindfulness were incorporated into every meeting you attend at work *and* in your personal life. Being focused means working more effectively. Working more effectively means having more time in your day for things you enjoy. All of this comes from making the decision to be more present.

In truth, it's not essential you follow these suggestions precisely. What is important is that you take time to think about your meeting experience and proactively look at what you can change to get more from your time with other people—for your benefit and theirs. To learn more about the power of Presence look at Strategy #1 in Part II.

The next technique will examine how you can use mindfulness principles to enhance focus and clarity in how you set goals.

Tips and Reflections for Mindful Meetings

- Reflect for a moment on meetings in your work environment. How effective are they? What can you do to help make better use of your time?
- The key guidelines for applying mindfulness to enhance meeting effectiveness are to give yourself time to mentally prepare for a meeting, ensure you and everyone else maintain presence during the meeting, and decisively end the meeting so that you can move on.
- Practicing mindfulness before, during, and after meetings enhances your ability to maintain focus and awareness and let go of distractions—and increases your training time!

TECHNIQUE #3

Goals

We All Have Goals

There are personal goals and professional goals. There are goals we're consciously aware of and work to define, but there are also goals that emanate from our subconscious and drive our behavior beyond our conscious awareness. Like lighthouses on the shore, our goals show us the way, even when the waves of life are big and a storm is blowing all around us.

Mindfulness and goals go well together. In fact, successfully achieving one is hard without the other. When you have clear goals, it's far easier to stay focused and aware. Similarly, when you're focused and aware, it's easier to keep your actions aligned with your goals. When you're in the second quadrant of the Matrix (see Figure T3.1), you'll find yourself more aligned with and focused on your goals. In any of the other quadrants, it can be very difficult to maintain clear goals.

Of course, achieving goals isn't always easy. Many obstacles can get in the way. This technique, presents mindful approaches to reaching your goals. But before diving into the criteria for mindful goal setting, let's examine how subconscious judgments can prevent you from achieving goals.

Why We Don't Achieve Our Goals

How many times have you made a New Year's resolution? Exercise more. Sleep more. Eat less. Or maybe even to start mindfulness training. Every

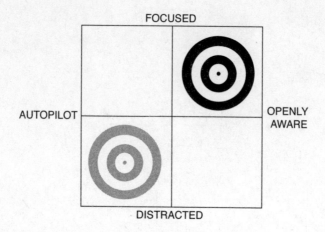

Figure T3.1   Clear goals and the Matrix.

time January 1 comes around, you resolve to change your life for the better. Yet despite clearly seeing the benefits, you still somehow manage to break your resolution. Why? What goes wrong? To answer that question, we need to understand a bit more about how our mind works.

Our mind operates simultaneously on conscious and subconscious levels. Many of our subconscious processes are rooted in the reptilian and limbic parts of our brain—the foundations for our survival instincts and the center of our emotions. Our conscious processes—like language, problem solving, and creativity—operate mainly in our cortex.

While our brain can consciously process around seven bits, or pieces, of information per second, it's nothing compared to the 11 million bits our subconscious handles in the same amount of time. This means there's much more happening beneath the surface of our conscious mind than we're aware of (see Figure T3.2).

When you make a New Year's resolution, you make it consciously. And while you might think that the seven bits per second your conscious mind can handle should be enough to follow through and achieve the goal, the reality is that in daily life you're constantly bombarded with distractions that require conscious attention. Many a great resolution can get drowned in this sea of distractions.

Besides the competition for conscious attention, your subconscious may be another barrier to achieving your goals. While your New Year's

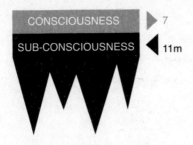

Figure T3.2 Conscious versus subconscious processing.

resolution makes sense for your conscious mind, subconscious processes may take you in another direction.

Take daily mindfulness training. Your conscious mind knows that training will ultimately help your focus, clarity, well-being, and physical health. But your subconscious often has other ideas. Maybe you have a deep-seated belief that the training won't work for you. Maybe you're afraid what others might think. Maybe you just don't believe mindfulness is beneficial, despite all data and testimonials to the contrary. All of these doubts, potentially backed by the power of 11 million bits per second of processing power, push you in a different direction than your conscious resolution to sit and train.

When it comes to maintaining clear goals, it's important to manage both our conscious mind and our subconscious processes. Our subconscious is primarily driven by two simple motivations: grasping for things we like and avoiding things we don't like. While our subconscious often craves short-term gratification, our conscious goals more often include delayed gratification.

The big question: how can we rein in the need for the subconscious mind to grasp or avoid to better maintain clarity around our goals?

Keeping Goals Front and Center

The more mindful you are, the more bandwidth of conscious attention you have. Mindfulness increases the number of conscious bits you can process. At the same time, it gives you a better awareness of what's happening in your subconscious mind. Mindfulness allows you to better align your conscious goals with your subconscious processes, keeping your goals center stage and enhancing your chances of success.

Still, knowing something is beneficial to us doesn't make us automatically do it. In our hectic and fast-paced reality, our minds tend to get cluttered. Even with extensive mindfulness training, the powerful processes of our subconscious can still overrule our conscious goals.

When you find your conscious goals slipping away from you, try the following steps for on-the-spot, mindful goal orientation. They take less than a minute.

Mindful Goal Orientation

- When you find yourself behaving counter to your goals, take a mindful pause (Figure T3.3)—focus on your breath as you calm down, gaining focus and clarity. This establishes your awareness.
- Ask yourself the question "What stories, beliefs, or grasping or avoidance is keeping me from doing the thing that moves me closer to my goal?"
- Whatever you find, face it and dismantle it by being present with it.
- Adjust your behavior and move on.

Figure T3.3   Mindful goal orientation.

Beyond keeping your goals in focus, the way you set goals can play a big role in your ability to achieve them. Two simple techniques can help you more effectively communicate goals to your subconscious: make sure your goals are specific, and frame them in a positive way.

Mindful Goal Setting

Clearly defined and specific goals are easier for your subconscious to understand. While the subconscious has amazing processing power, it's not the most organized. Just think of the last dream you remember—was it scrambled or clear? logical or a bit chaotic? This is a reflection of the processes in your subconscious.

If you set a broad goal simply "to do mindfulness training every day," your subconscious may not get the message. What does that mean? For how many minutes? Where? When? How? Defining the same goal more specifically greatly increases your chances of success: *First thing every morning, I will do mindfulness training for 10 minutes, on the couch, in my living room, following the instructions in Chapter 2 for training sharp focus.* With this kind of goal, the message to the subconscious is clear and concrete.

Positively framing your goals also makes it easier for your subconscious to process them. By default, the subconscious moves toward the desirable and away from the unpleasant. Whereas a negatively framed goal might be *I want to avoid multitasking*, the positive version is *I want to focus on one task at a time.* With the second framing, you're clearly moving toward something positive—and the processing power of your subconscious mind can help you get there.

All the focus and framing in the world won't help you decide what kind of goals you should set or at what point you should let them go.

Hold Your Goals Lightly

Jose, a senior manager at a global American pharmaceutical and consumer goods company, was great at achieving his goals. He had worked hard for many years to reach a senior position in the company. He was humbly proud of his achievement and enjoyed the benefits. He shared with me his story of the hard work, long hours, and cancelled vacations it had required. It had taken many busy years, involving periods of personal and professional challenge, but he had been steadfast. He had a goal and he had held it tightly.

In hindsight, however, he realized there had been some irreversible costs to holding on to this goal. Due to years of stress, his health was failing, his children were not as close to him as he would have liked, and his divorce two years earlier was still a source of regret.

So the question became, was the senior position worth it?

In *Seven Habits of Highly Effective People*, Steven Covey asked, "What is the point of reaching the top of the ladder, to find that it was placed against the wrong wall?"

Jose had reached the top of his ladder. He had a great career, money, and respect. But with his focus on professional recognition and success, he had lost sight of other important aspects of his life.

Many of us hold on to our goals too tightly. In other words, we fixate on a goal so much that we lose perspective; we cede control to the goal. Learning to hold our goals lightly, and let go of them if they won't bring us long-term happiness, is an important skill.

Goals are important—and often hard to achieve. With a mind that's focused and clear, setting and reaching our goals becomes much easier, as does letting go of those goals that may turn out to be detrimental to our happiness.

The next technique will explore ways mindfulness can help you achieve your goals through mindfully managing priorities.

Tips and Reflections for Clear Goals

- Clear goals help us be more focused and aware of what's important to us; mindfulness helps us apply more focus and awareness to realizing our goals.
- Subconscious processes can get in the way of realizing our goals. But with greater awareness, they can be leveraged to help us.
- Focus is important, but blind. Combining focus with awareness, as is done in the quadrant two of The Matrix of Mental Effectiveness, ensures we don't blindly focus on goals.
- Take a moment to write down your key goals for your professional life and for your personal life. Make them specific and positively framed to increase your potential for success.

TECHNIQUE #4

Priorities

Whether personal or professional, goals are important. However, not all goals are created equal. To be successful, we need to be able to prioritize which goals are most important.

Managing priorities allows us to keep what's important in focus and better maintain balance when goals inevitably conflict. When applied to managing priorities, mindfulness can help us declutter our minds and focus on fewer things. With greater awareness, we can ensure we're turning our attention toward the "right" tasks or objectives: the ones that enable us to get results.

A common management framework, the 80/20 principle—also known as the Pareto principle—proposes that 80 percent of our time and effort goes into activities that only generate 20 percent of outcomes. This means we spend the majority of our time on activities that produce a proportionally small amount of results.

Ideally, instead we should focus on activities that generate that other 80 percent of our desired outcomes. Take a moment to think about the kind of activities at work that take up a large amount of your time compared to the results they produce. Then, think about the activities that take up less time for greater outcomes.

When we're more focused and aware, we spend our time on the activities that generate the greatest return for the least effort (see Figure T4.1).

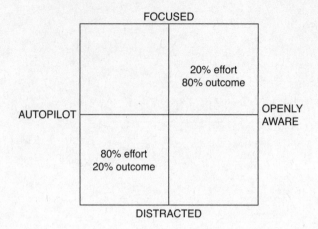

Figure T4.1 The 80/20 Principle and the Matrix.

When we're distracted, when we're on autopilot, it's easy to do lot of "busywork" that takes a lot of time, but delivers few results.

This technique examines the different ways mindfulness can help you manage your priorities. It presents the phenomenon of "action addition"—one of the root causes of poor prioritization—and describes ways to avoid it. It also includes an exploration on how slowing down can actually be an effective way of speeding up.

Clear Priorities or Spinning Your Wheels?

One large-scale study on prioritizing work, conducted by the Franklin Covey Institute, looked at the workplace activities of over 350,000 people. What they found was that most people spend an average of 41 percent on low-priority activities as opposed to priorities that are truly pressing.[1]

That study was not an anomaly.

In 2012, London Business School professors observed managers at Sony, Lufthansa, and LG Electronics to try to learn about the ability of managers to prioritize tasks. According to the *Harvard Business Review* article, "Beware the Busy Manager,"[2] they came to the following conclusion: "Very few [managers] use their time as effectively as they could. They think they're attending to pressing matters, but they're really just spinning their wheels."

It turns out, being busy doesn't necessarily equate to being effective.

When we shared this research with a global Japanese technology and consumer goods giant, they recognized the issue immediately. One leader shared his experience: "I get that rejecting the noise will give me the mental clarity and calm to be more effective. But in reality, it's not that easy. Quite often, I find that I'm so overwhelmed with information and distractions that I just jump on whatever feels most pressing in the moment. It's like an impulse that's hard to control."

Sound familiar?

There are many reasons why people have trouble staying focused on the kinds of tasks that produce the greatest outcomes. When the mind's under pressure—when it never gets a break from being bombarded with information and distractions—it can be difficult to maintain focus, let alone prioritize tasks. With a mind under siege, it's almost impossible to keep the few truly crucial activities front and center.

Giving in to the urge to act because we're under pressure is all too common. Many of us are prone to waste precious time simply because we follow impulses: we don't have that one-second edge necessary to think through the consequences of automatically jumping to a task just because it "feels" urgent.

In many ways, we're actually addicted to the action itself. We're dependent on the need to accomplish something—send off an e-mail, reply to a request, tackle a new problem—regardless of whether it best serves our intended objectives or designated goals.

Action Addiction

Addiction to action is one of the biggest threats to mental effectiveness and productivity. The root cause of action addiction is an untrained mind. A well-trained mind is the only way to overcome it. In this section we look more closely at the phenomenon of action addiction and how it can be overcome. Let's start by visualizing what a typical morning might look like for someone working in a PAID reality. We will call him Jim.

At 8:30 a.m. Jim gets into the office. After a good night's rest, his mind is fairly clear and he has a good sense of the most important priorities for the day—the activities that will take 20 percent effort and deliver 80 percent outcome.

On the way to his desk, Jim passes a number of colleagues. One colleague stops him to ask his opinion on a burning issue. Even though the issue itself doesn't fall within the scope of Jim's priorities for the day, he wants to help out. He takes some time to offer his best answer.

Appreciating the help, his colleague thanks him saying, "Jim, you're the man!"

Jim then gets a pleasant kick of the neurotransmitter dopamine. The instant gratification of finishing something—*anything*—overruled Jim's high-priority activities for the moment.

Once he arrives at his desk, Jim opens his e-mail. Within minutes, a multitude of questions and requests seem to require immediate action. Deep down, Jim knows many of these issues belong to the group of tasks that take 80 percent of his effort and produce 20 percent of his outcomes.

But—the urge to jump into action again overrules greater priorities. The impulse to immediately react wins over the wisdom of thoughtfully managing his time. Jim starts answering e-mails, receiving a fresh kick of dopamine every time he hits "send." Due to an untrained mind, action addiction takes over Jim's day and usurps the great intentions and important priorities from the morning.

If Jim's scenario sounds familiar, you're not alone.

When we're under pressure, our brain hijacks some of our higher cognitive functions, putting us into survival mode. As a result, we tend to rush toward instant gratification—the things we can control or accomplish right this second. We become addicted to the action itself, as presented in Figure T4.2.

When we're addicted to action, we do things not because they're important, but because we want to feel important. The tasks are in front of us, and we want to be useful and productive. The problem is, when we don't step back to ensure we're spending time on tasks aligned with our main goals, we end up wasting a lot of time on immediate— though often inessential—tasks.

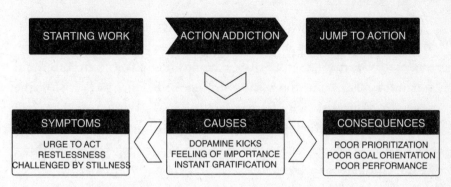

Figure T4.2 The symptoms, causes, and consequences of action addiction.

Action addiction is one of the biggest threats to our mental effectiveness and productivity. To gauge your own level of action addiction, try taking the following test.

Test Your Action Addiction

- When you arrive at your desk, just as you are about to get started, sit down and look out the window or into your blank computer screen.
- Don't act. Don't talk. Don't solve a problem. Just sit and do nothing for three minutes.
- If you're challenged by the inactivity, you are likely experiencing some degree of action addiction.

Action addiction takes away your ability to maintain clear priorities and work toward your most important goals. It hampers your performance and effectiveness. But don't worry. There are mindful ways to avoid action addiction.

Avoiding Action Addiction

While action addiction is a natural outcome of modern, fast-paced work environments, it doesn't need to be a constant impediment. Action addiction can be counteracted through formal mindfulness training, as well as through being mindful when priorities conflict.

The neurotransmitter called serotonin produced in the brain during mindfulness training balances the dopamine kick action addition creates. To learn more about the relationship between serotonin and dopamine, read about the mental strategy of Balance in Part II of the book. And through more formal mindfulness training—as described in Part III—we become physically less attached or addicted to certain behaviors. We gain more mental freedom and strength in everything we do, especially at work.

While mindfulness training can give you the mental freedom and strength needed to better avoid action addiction in general terms, you may still find yourself with many demands on your attention and time. What should you do when you experience conflicting priorities?

Choice Points—When Priorities Conflict

Conflicting priorities are the most common causes of action addiction. When two or more priorities conflict, you reach a choice point: a point at which you need to decide how to best manage multiple priorities or competing urgencies.

We often react to choice points by jumping into action. There it is again, that action addiction. But, as you now know, not all action is aligned with our goals. Thankfully, there is a simple way to train your mind to avoid the trap of action addiction when confronted with conflicting priorities (see Figure T4.3).

When priorities conflict, take a breath before you jump into action. Endure the discomfort of conflicting priorities. Take a brief pause to

Figure T4.3 Mindfully resolving conflicting priorities.

recall your priorities and then make a decision based on your overarching goals. If you find the newly arrived task should take precedence, follow the second rule of mental effectiveness—choosing your distractions mindfully—and direct your full attention to the new task.

If you determine the new task shouldn't take precedence, just say "no" and adhere to the first rule of mental effectiveness—focus on what you choose. More often than not, this "no" is an internal response and not directed toward a colleague or manager. With the ever-increasing stream of information and complexity coming our way, a well-considered "no" becomes more and more necessary.

Although it may sound simple, taking a breath to recall your priorities can be difficult. When faced with multiple tasks, doing nothing but breathing may trigger restlessness or even anxiety. But with practice, you can overcome this automatic reaction to conflicting priorities. You can gain one second of mental freedom to get ahead of your impulses. One simple breath, repeated several times, can make the difference between action addiction and a well-trained mind.

Some people may say, "If I have to take a conscious breath every time priorities conflict, it'll take me all day to get anything done." The solution to this problem is to learn how to speed up by slowing down.

Speed Up by Slowing Down

How can slowing down possibly help you speed up? Consider the fastest land animal on the planet, the cheetah.

The cheetah has been recorded running at speeds of up to 120 kilometers (about 75 miles) per hour. Yet, if the cheetah were to run at that pace for a full day, it would be dead from exhaustion in just hours. For the cheetah to use its full speed while hunting most effectively, it starts very slowly. At first, it slowly stalks its prey, blood engorging its muscles and its brain maintaining a singular focus. This brief phase of calm actually enables the cheetah to explode into action when its prey is within range.

Taking one breath when priorities conflict is not unlike the cheetah beginning its hunt. By taking a brief pause, you're able to maintain your focus and awareness. This allows you to respond to situations with the most appropriate action—to concentrate on your priorities and goals—rather than simply acting on autopilot. The next technique, Planning, takes prioritization one step further.

Tips and Reflections for Mindfully Managing Priorities

- Clear priorities help you focus on the right things and enable you to be more fully present and clear minded.
- Mindfulness helps you avoid action addiction and enables you to act based on your priorities.
- Take a moment to reflect on your own experience with doing low-value activities and/or being addicted to action.
- What one thing can you do tomorrow to decrease action addiction?

TECHNIQUE #5

Planning

We are constant planners—whether we realize it or not. We make plans intentionally and involuntarily. We are overloaded with information, and the mind often goes on autopilot and plans and plans and plans. We get absorbed in action addiction and keep spinning our wheels—at the cost of real planning.

Real planning is about overcoming action addiction, cultivating mental effectiveness, and executing on your priorities. Real planning requires slowing down, so that you can speed up. It's an investment in time up front that has significant payback down the road. In this technique we look at how mindfulness can be a foundation for effective planning.

Mindful Planning in the Present

Elaine, a senior human resource executive at one of the largest banks in America, explained the challenges of clear planning this way: "I remember I used to be quite present and calm when I was younger. I remember I slept well at night. I remember how I could read a book for hours without being mentally distracted. Nowadays, I find myself constantly busy in my mind. At night I often wake up, planning for the next day. When trying to read a book, I hardly finish a page before realizing I am busy with planning for tomorrow. And even when I need to plan something, I find my mind occupied with so many other things, that it is difficult to make a good plan."

We have all been there. We have all felt overwhelmed by responsibilities at some point and unable to figure out how to fit it all in. With the information overload of our busy lives, our mind is primed to be on the move, always thinking ten steps ahead, conducting nonstop planning on autopilot.

Like Elaine, our mind wants to plan even when we try to sleep. Instead of being focused on an important conversation, our mind starts planning what we'll have for lunch. It plans when we're in meetings, writing e-mails, and commuting. It plans when we're just trying to relax at home.

It's like we're master planners—but somehow we've lost the master plan.

When under pressure, we think we need to plan to survive. The fact is, though, we can survive without constant planning. We may actually live better and get more done if we tone down the automatic planning, do more mindful planning, and focus on what's truly important.

While mindful planning is both built on our experiences from the past and directed toward the future (see Figure T5.1), it's always done in the present moment. Therefore, mindful planning is about deciding *when* to plan, rather than simply planning on autopilot.

Clear planning makes it easier for you to live a more mindful life, and mindfulness, in turn, helps you plan more clearly. In this sense, clear planning and mindfulness are complementary, both helping to keep you in quadrant 2 of The Matrix of Mental Effectiveness, as depicted in Figure T5.2.

While this all makes sense in theory, the question now becomes one of execution. Automatic, unfocused planning is the result of an untrained mind, a mind that involuntarily wanders between the past and future without fixing on the present. To plan clearly, being present in the here and now is absolutely critical.

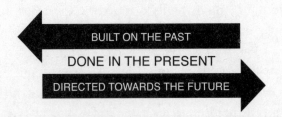

BUILT ON THE PAST

DONE IN THE PRESENT

DIRECTED TOWARDS THE FUTURE

Figure T5.1   Mindful planning.

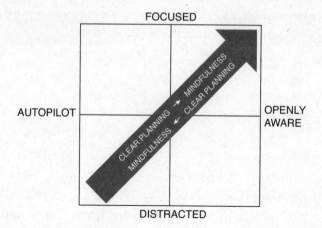

Figure T5.2   Mindful planning and the Matrix.

Being present in the moment doesn't require a change in the actual things you do or the way you live your life; rather, it's a change in *how* you pay attention. Being present in the moment is a conscious decision.

Make the Time to Plan

There's an old expression that goes, "The bad news is, time flies: the good news is, you're the pilot."

Yes, time flies—particularly when we're busy and especially when we're overloaded. Conducting clear planning every day can help each and every one of us become better pilots.

It will also make us more mindful.

Time flies especially fast when we feel like we lack control. And we're not in control if we suffer from action addiction. When compelled by any addiction, we're not free to think clearly or act rationally. Instead, we're driven by a force that feels stronger than our will. We're driven not by choice, but by the urge.

This urge often strikes when we first get to work. We allow it to pull us directly into action—any action. In acting, we're immediately rewarded with a rush of dopamine and a general sense of having done something of value.

It feels good.

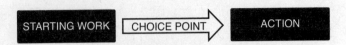

Figure T5.3   The choice point.

The downside, of course, is that we blind ourselves to the bigger picture. Our goals and priorities become subservient to immediate actions. We're at a choice point, as reflected in Figure T5.3.

Too often, instead of moving forward through intentional action, we end up stuck in place: working, acting, trying, but not making any real progress. The morning is the most important choice point of the day. As it sets the tone for the rest of the day, it's critical to begin the morning with a period of clear planning.

Planning Your Day

When you take the time to plan your day, you gain peace and quiet by knowing that time has been reserved for major priorities. You're better able to maintain control and avoid the temptation of being controlled by distractions. It's a small investment with a big return. Here's how to clearly and mindfully plan your day.

Clear Planning on a Daily Basis

When you get to work, make a habit of reserving the first ten minutes to do the following:

- Do one to two minutes of ABCD mindfulness training (see Chapter 2) to enhance your focus and subdue the impulse of action addiction.
- Make a short list of the highest priority activities of the day—or review a list you made at the end of the previous day.
- Plan your calendar for the day according to the highest priorities.
- Now, get to work.
- Review your plan once or twice during the day to track your progress.

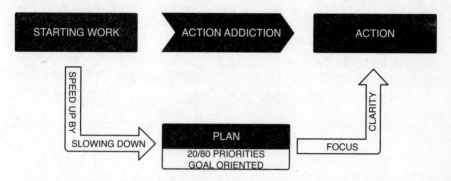

Figure T5.4   Daily mindful planning.

Now, a daily session of mindful, clear planning may initially feel like it's slowing you down. But, as explained in the previous technique, slowing down can be an effective way of speeding up. Starting the day with focus and clarity allows you to work more effectively than simply following each and every distraction that arises (see Figure T5.4). By working more effectively, you'll be amazed at how much time you gain.

Putting effort into clear planning keeps your coworkers or other distractions from hijacking your time.

Mindful planning has applications beyond just organizing your day. Weekly and monthly planning sessions can help you keep the big picture in mind and manage your calendar accordingly.

Principles for Mindful Scheduling

While there are some general principles for how to mindfully schedule your time, how you apply them will be determined by your working style and company culture. First and foremost, remember the 80/20 rule as described in the previous technique on Priorities.

Keeping this rule in mind, allocate most of your time to completing activities that deliver the greatest outcomes for the least amount of effort. Consider what proportion of your daily calendar you can realistically reserve for these tasks, while still leaving time for the urgent matters that will inevitably crop up. How much time you set aside for urgent matters depends on the nature of your work. Whatever you decide, saving a realistic margin of unscheduled time can help you avoid being put under unnecessary pressure.

Besides planning out your priorities and setting aside time for putting out fires, also consider how much time you need to recharge your mental batteries every day—whether through small breaks, a short walk, or your ten minutes of mindfulness training. Finally, make sure to reserve time for unavoidable "transition" activities, such as follow-up communication after meetings and travel. The following is a summary of the mindful work schedule.

The Mindful Work Schedule

To summarize, the principles for handling your work schedule include

- allocating time for high-priority activities;
- allocating time for preparation;
- determining how much time you should leave free for urgent matters;
- planning time for recharging your batteries;
- planning your lunch; and
- planning for transition activities, such as meeting follow-up and travel.

Just as clear planning can help you reach your professional goals, it can do the same in your personal life. Think about dedicating quality, one-on-one time to being with your children or setting aside an evening with your partner or a close friend. Think about the kinds of activities you need to do for yourself to stay happy and healthy. Personally, I go to a mindfulness retreat at least once a year because I know it's crucial to my ability to help others find calm and realize their potential. If you don't dedicate time to reflecting on your goals and priorities, time will fly by on autopilot. You'll feel out of control, with precious moments slipping away. But by mindfully planning, you'll achieve greater success at work and at home. You'll use each moment well.

Which is good, because it won't come again.

The next technique explores another means of making the best use of each moment—specifically those moments that you are interacting with other people where the application of mindful communication can be of great value.

Tips and Reflections for Mindful Planning

- Mindful planning is a great antidote to action addiction.
- Reflect on your own experience with planning. Do you recognize a tendency to plan on autopilot and think about issues that aren't relevant in the here and now?
- Mindful planning is built on the past, directed toward the future, but done in the present.
- Consider ways you can be more mindful—more focused and aware—in terms of when and how you plan your time.

TECHNIQUE #6

Communication

There is a great quote often attributed to former chairman of the Federal Reserve Alan Greenspan, "I know you think you understand what you thought I said but I'm not sure you realize that what you heard is not what I meant."[1]

Got that?

Sending a message is not the same as communicating a message. For effective communication to occur, the receiver must understand what the sender intended—not just hear or read the words.

Effective communication can be difficult, but it doesn't have to be. With a calm, clear mind and good intentions by both parties in the communication, it can be relatively easy to ensure even difficult messages are sent, received, and understood.

The foundation of mindful communication is, as in many other aspects of life, being fully present in your interactions with other people. Only when we're fully present do we get the most out of our time together. And only when we're fully present can we be sure to understand what's actually being communicated. This technique explores the barriers to effective communication and provides simple steps to enhance listening and speaking with mindfulness. But to begin, let's look at the importance of empathy and external awareness with respect to effective communication.

Empathy and External Awareness

Empathy—being in tune with the feelings of others—plays a major role in effective communication. If you have a sense of how the person with whom you're trying to communicate feels, it's easier to get on their wavelength.

Fundamentally, empathy is based on the development of external awareness, one of the key outcomes of mindfulness training. External awareness includes the ability to sense and read other people's state of mind, as well as be aware of the ways in which you can influence or help them. Instructions on how to enhance internal and external awareness are described in Chapter 3 on Open Awareness.

From a neurological perspective, two fundamental tendencies in the human mind create barriers to effective communication. First, there's the reality of the mind's natural tendency to wander, as discussed in Chapter 1.

The second tendency is our mind's orientation to see things as we expect to see them, commonly known as habitual perception. This orientation is discussed in detail in Strategy 4—Beginner's Mind. But briefly, habitual perception, or cognitive rigidity as it's also known—is the mind's natural desire to place reality into simple, pre-existing categories. This causes us to believe the mind's own limited projections about other people, ourselves, and all the things we encounter. Thus we are being cognitively rigid when we limit our perceptions. Both our wandering minds and this rigidity severely hinder our ability to communicate.

Are You Listening?

When I came home late from work one evening, one of my boys was waiting for me. He clearly wanted my attention. He was upset about something that had happened at school and wanted to talk to me about it.

So I sat down and asked him to tell me what happened.

While he was speaking, my mind kept wandering to the meeting I just had, the e-mails piling up in my inbox, a long report I had to read, and the dinner that still needed to be cooked.

Being a clever and empathic boy, it didn't take him long to recognize that I wasn't giving him my full attention. "Dad, you're not listening," he said.

My automatic reaction was to blurt out, "Yes, I am. I'm here in front of you, aren't I?"

At that moment, however, I realized that I had assumed he was telling me about the same concerns he usually had a school and that there was nothing new.

It was a classic case of ineffective communication. The truth was, I wasn't paying attention to him. My mind was wandering, and my ability to listen was blocked by my habitual perception of him. What's more, when he asked for my attention, my impulse was reactive rather than responsive. With a clearer, more open mind, I could have gotten one second ahead of my immediate reaction and habitual perception. Then I would have seen an upset child who simply needed his father's undivided attention.

We all have minds that wander. We all get trapped by our habitual perceptions. We've all had the experience of assuming we know what someone will say before they say it. But making that assumption can undercut communication before it even has a chance to begin. Perhaps something new will be said, maybe even something valuable.

Mindful communication is based on avoiding both a wandering mind and your habitual perception. Because of this, it's a terrific way to train yourself to be more present and open minded in general.

In terms of The Matrix of Mental Effectiveness (see Figure T6.1), effective communication happens at the intersection of sharp focus and open awareness. In quadrant two of the matrix, we're focused enough to

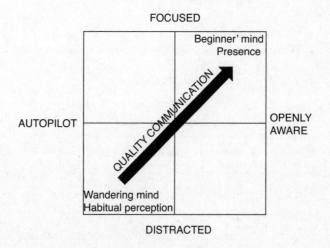

Figure T6.1 When mindful communication occurs.

tame our wandering minds and openly aware enough to overcome our habitual perception and cognitive rigidity. In this state, the key ingredients to effective communication—attention, empathy, understanding—are all present.

To communicate effectively, it's also important to realize that each communication has two equally important sides: listening and speaking.

Two Sides to Effective Communication

If someone is talking but no one is listening, well, that's not communication. It's as simple as that. The following are a few guidelines to help you enhance your communication with mindfulness, both while listening *and* while speaking.

Listen with Mindfulness

Simply put, listening with mindfulness involves giving your full attention to whomever is speaking. There are four guidelines for listening with this type of focus. We use the acronym STOP—be Silent, Tuned in, Open, and Present (see Figure T6.2)—to make it easy to remember these guidelines.

Figure T6.2   Listening mindfully.

Here's how to put STOP into practice.

Listening with STOP

- Be Silent. Being silent means not talking. In other words, it means switching off your external voice. It also means switching off your internal voice. Listening fully to the other person requires complete attention.

- Tune In. Create a connection between your body language and your intentions. Use gestures to indicate you are present. Something as simple as a smile can communicate your presence to another person.
- Be Open. Switch off any habitual perception you may have. Assume the other person has a good reason for speaking and something valuable to communicate.
- Be Present. Be fully present as long as you're interacting with the other person. Consciously bring your attention back every time your thoughts wander. Use the person you're with as an anchor for your attention. In this way, you're giving them the gift of your presence and also training your mind to be more present.

Speaking with Mindfulness

There are ways to apply mindfulness when you're the one talking, as well. We use the acronym ACT to present key qualities for speaking with mindfulness—be Appropriate, Compassionate, and Timed (see Figure T6.3).

Figure T6.3   Speaking mindfully.

To implement ACT while speaking with another person, follow these guidelines.

Speaking with ACT

- Be Appropriate. Say the right words, to the right person, at the right time. Put another way, ensure what you're saying is useful and beneficial to the other person in this moment. As the Greek philosopher and mathematician Pythagoras said, "Keep quiet. Or say something better than silence."

- Be Compassionate. Speak with a desire to contribute to the other person's well-being. We want to be of benefit to others. But understand, being compassionate doesn't mean keeping quiet when someone's made a mistake. In fact, providing people with constructive feedback on their actions can be very compassionate; it can help them learn, develop, and grow.

- Be Timed. Say what has to be said and no more. Don't ramble on, but also don't cut it so short you never make it to your point. Say what needs to be said, and then stop.

In essence, mindful communication is about getting the most out of your interactions with other people. Through effective communication, you can contribute to common objectives, have more fulfilling relationships, and enhance the well-being of others.

Try it for yourself.

Every time you communicate with another person, listen with STOP and speak with ACT. And always be sure to ask yourself, "How can I be of greatest benefit to this person in this moment?"

Don't just take my word for it, though. Consider the case of a global brand management and consulting firm. The Australian senior leadership team introduced a mindfulness program for the entire office. A key objective for them was to enhance teamwork, collaboration, and specifically communication.

Some of the staff were skeptical at first, but after a couple of weeks people started noticing small changes in how they interacted with each other. People were generally more calm, more considerate, more kind, more focused, and overall much nicer and easier to work with.

When asked which work application benefited the group the most, Dominic, the managing director, said that people started bringing postcards with "S T O P" and "A C T" to meetings, and it helped them remember to be more mindful of how they interacted with each other.

"Those cards were a real turning point for the staff as it helped us break out of some of our negative patterns of ineffective communication and enabled us to work much better together."

Communication is fundamental to the success of any organization. Much of our success at work depends on how well we're able to engage with our colleagues, employees, supervisors, customers, and suppliers. We need to both hear them and influence them, understand them and guide them. Bringing mindfulness into all professional and person interactions is a powerful way to accomplish this more consistently and more effectively.

Next, we will look beyond the use of mindfulness to enhance performance and effectiveness and explore the application of mindfulness to increase creativity.

Tips and Reflections for Mindful Communication

- There are two fundamental barriers to effective communication: the wandering mind and habitual perception. Learn to recognize when either—or both—barriers are hampering your communication.
- To enhance your ability to listen with mindfulness, STOP—be Silent, Tuned-in, Open, and Present.
- To enhance your ability to speak with mindfulness, ACT—be Appropriate, Compassionate, and Timed.
- Choose an interaction over the next week and intentionally apply STOP and ACT. Consider the difference it makes.

Creativity

This technique explores the relationship between mindfulness and creativity including a formula for enhancing creating thinking. Without creative and innovative ideas, the chances of an organization being successful in the long term are not good. Yet, being creative and innovative is getting more and more difficult.

Researcher Kyung Hee Kim at the College of William & Mary analyzed 300,000 creativity test scores of both children and adults taken over the past 50 years. What Kim found was that creativity scores peaked in 1990, and then started to steadily decline.[1]

There are many theories about what might be causing such a dip in creativity, but there's no clear reason for the drop. Regardless of the cause, to successfully address the challenges we face in today's expanding marketplace, we all need to enhance our ability to think creatively.

In this technique, I'll explore the relationship between mindfulness and creativity as well as provide a formula for enhancing creative thinking. But first, let's look at some of the most common barriers to creativity.

What Stops Us from Thinking Creatively?

David Ogilvy, founder of global advertising firm Ogilvy & Mather, had a saying: "Sell or else." From hawking kitchen appliances on the street to running a global enterprise, he never lost sight of this goal. But the demands of maintaining a viable business combined with the need for on-command creative performance resulted in an eternal catch 22. Often, commerce and creativity don't mix well.

Mary-Ann, a European Country director for a global American advertising and branding agency, introduced corporate mindfulness with the aim of enhancing both creativity and business effectiveness within her staff. As with most advertising companies, a "now-culture" pervaded the office environment. Clients constantly demanded high-quality creative ideas—*now*.

Pressure to be creative, especially on short notice, is tough.

On the one hand, Mary-Ann knew her team needed to improve their overall effectiveness to get projects done as quickly as possible, while on the other hand, she knew they also needed the mental space necessary to think outside the box.

The entire team signed up for the mindfulness program. Over a six-month period, they practiced together, slowly redefining how they worked both as individuals and collectively. One of their most important realizations was the fact that managing attention is vital to creativity.

In other words, if your mind wanders, it's almost impossible to be creative.

Based on this discovery, the team created internal guidelines for when team members could be disturbed and when they needed to be given space to focus. As the months passed, the culture changed. Once hectic, the group as a whole settled down. People became calmer, more focused, and more effective, and had more mental space for being creative.

Specifically, they looked at how mindfulness could apply to their process for creating a new ad campaign. In the past, their meetings could often become very heated as people became passionate about their own ideas or approaches.

A few weeks into the training program, they decided to take more intentional pauses throughout these meetings to give people the opportunity to relax and release any of the attachment they had to one idea or another. They found that these mini mindfulness training sessions throughout their meetings made the session more effective and quite often produced more creative ideas than when they would just push through.

One of the challenges of being creative in today's fast-paced world is not that we don't think enough. Most people think a lot.

The issue, actually, is the opposite: many people aren't able to stop thinking. They can't let go of thoughts and distractions long enough to open their minds to truly creative ideas. In a world that's always "on," it's not always easy to turn "off."

Our tendency to think about problems and issues in habitual ways is one of the main barriers to creativity. Often, we choose solutions that we're familiar with or that have already produced success. This familiarity makes it difficult to break free of our regular mental algorithms, our normal patterns of thought. This concept is explored further in Strategy 4—Beginner's Mind. For now, though, just understand that our typical response to most problems is to ruminate. And then ruminate some more, spinning through the same issues without generating any new or fresh ideas.

To break this natural tendency, we simply need to stop.

For a second.

Just long enough to let our synapses fire and our limbic, or subconscious, brain to take over. You see, creativity comes from tapping into the potential ideas outside our limited conscious awareness.

Activating the Subconscious

Pablo Picasso clearly had a gift for seeing objects and people in unique ways. But his natural ability was not something he simply took for granted.

For him, creativity and new ways of thinking were qualities to consciously strengthen through simple actions. Picasso had a specific process for encouraging creative solutions. To start, he would extensively research the area in which he wanted to work, without forcing any of the information to align with preconceived ideas. After a period of study and research, he set the books aside and took a bath.

Yes. A bath.

By having a bath, Picasso could activate the power of his subconscious. In essence, by letting go of thinking—a conscious process—he was able to tap into a greater source of potential ideas. He created an open connection between his subconscious and conscious mind.

To tap into your subconscious, much like Picasso, follow these four steps: (1) formulate the problem; (2) let go of the problem; (3) allow time; and (4) activate.

Step 1: Formulate the Problem

The subconscious doesn't operate logically or rationally. If you want its help, you have to give it a simple and clear problem. Take a moment to think about what's at the core of your challenge as well as what the ideal result would be. Then write down a pointed question about what you specifically need. For example: "What's a suitable structure for this report?" Or, "Who can help me to get moving with this case?" Or, "What's the fundamental reason for this conflict?"

Once you have the problem clearly defined, let it go.

Step 2: Let Go of the Problem

It's crucial to let go of the problem and the desire for a solution. If you don't let go of the problem—if you carry on thinking about it—your conscious brain will block any subconscious activity. And that will ruminate and keep you from finding a new solution.

Instead, take the piece of paper with your question on it and put it away. But be sure you know where it is: you'll need to take it out again later. This gives your consciousness the peace and quiet needed to let go.

Step 3: Allow Time

Time is now on your side. You've let the problem drop like a fishing line into your subconscious while you happily carry on with your usual business. A number of activities can encourage the process. While Picasso found taking a bath to be effective in letting go of mental clutter, something entirely different may work for you. What's crucial is that the activity makes it easy for you to let go of the problem. Four specific activities have shown themselves to be very effective: mindfulness training, power napping, physical activity, and sleep. Let's look at each one in more detail.

Mindfulness Training. A growing body of research shows clear links between mindfulness training and creativity.[2] Consciously letting go of all conscious thoughts and distractions—a key component of formal mindfulness training—facilitates a strong connection to your subconscious mind. If you've started a systematic mindfulness program, you may have already experienced moments of increased creativity during your training. If you haven't, keep in mind that Part III of this book outlines the practices and guidelines needed to start a self-directed mindfulness training regimen.

Power Napping. Power napping has also been shown to increase creativity. Once you've written out your problem and set it aside, allow yourself a three- to ten-minute power nap. After, test whether or not you were able to let go of the problem. If not, take another brief nap or try another activity.

Physical Activity. When you're physically active, it's easier to get out of your head and into an experiential mode. Take a walk. Go for a run. Go for a bike ride. Playing games like Ping-Pong or foosball can also help. Again, what's most crucial is that the activity helps you let go of the problem.

Sleep. The final activity is sleep. It goes without saying that sleep means that your conscious mind can't get in the way of the process. There are countless examples of fantastic ideas coming to people in the middle of a deep sleep. To make the best use of sleep, write down your problem and set it aside on your bedside table. Then follow the guidelines for Step 4, Activate, immediately when you wake up in the morning.

Step 4: Activate

You've now identified a problem, let it go, and given your subconscious time to work. The final task is to help your subconscious communicate with your conscious. While this sometimes happens without trying, it's also a process you can push through. Take a blank piece of paper and draw or write without trying to be specific. Give yourself time for the answer to take shape.

In this final stage, it can be valuable to ask yourself whether or not you're really ready to look at the problem with a fresh perspective. If you notice a flood of old information or old ideas coming into your mind, you may need more time to fully let the problem go. In this case, return to Step 3.

It Takes Time

Cultivating creativity and innovation in your subconscious takes time. At first, you might find it challenging and the results not very exciting. But the more you work at it—the more you strengthen the connection between your conscious and subconscious mind—the easier it becomes.

In general, by simplifying your life and your mind, you can strengthen your own creative flow. Switching off the radio while you're driving, reducing your screen time on the computer or in front of the television, getting more sleep, avoiding information overload—all of these simple adjustments can help you have a greater mental capacity for cultivating creativity and new ideas.

A full mind is like a full cup: if there's no room for anything new, new ideas will spill over the side and be wasted. As Dutch painter Hans Hoffmann said, "the ability to simplify means to eliminate the unnecessary so that the necessary may speak."[3] Research shows that simplicity in your working life equates to better creative flow.[4]

In this way, less truly is more.

Creativity in the Matrix

When we ask people where they believe creativity lands on The Matrix of Mental Effectiveness, as described in Chapter 1, the answer is most often in the fourth quadrant—the quadrant that *can* be openly aware, but easily distracted. The rationale is that in this quadrant the mind is open to new ideas. In some ways, this makes a lot of sense.

But the challenge with creativity isn't just coming up with new ideas. Creativity also requires us to hold on to the good ones, instead of letting them slip away in the stream of distraction. In other words, we create the right circumstances for creativity in the fourth quadrant, but we end up throwing out the baby with the bathwater because we can't focus.

Creative thinking, that is, the generation of creative ideas, can begin in the fourth quadrant, but for us to be able to capture, retain, and make use of these ideas, we need to be in quadrant two (see Figure T7.1). In the second quadrant, we're not only aware of when good ideas occur, but we also have the ability to hold on to them with focus so we can apply and execute them. What's most crucial in fourth quadrant is for our focus to be relaxed. Where a tense focus can shut off creative flow, a relaxed focus allows new, innovative ideas to surface.

It's probably safe to say that we would all love to be more creative, more capable of producing new and innovative ideas and insights. One of the real barriers to creativity is the fact that we're so busy. We don't feel we have enough time or energy to walk through each step in the process. But as many before you have discovered, it doesn't necessarily take a lot of time or major adjustments to your everyday life to cultivate creativity. With a few brief, but intentional changes, a more present, calm, and creative mind is well within your reach.

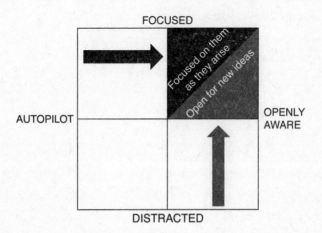

Figure T7.1   Creativity and the Matrix.

The generation of lots of new ideas can often result in change. Next, we will look at how mindfulness can help in managing change.

Tips and Reflections for Creativity

- Many work environments are not conducive to creativity—when we're under pressure and faced with ongoing distractions, it's hard to generate new ideas.
- Creative insights don't arise through thinking. Truly creative ideas come when we're not thinking and instead we're tapping into the power of our subconscious mind.
- Our subconscious mind experiences much more than we are consciously aware of—tapping into those experiences provides a wellspring of creative ideas.
- There are four steps in the creativity process: formulate, let go, give time, and activate. Give these a try to see how they work for you.

TECHNIQUE #8

Change

We've all heard the saying, "The only constant in life is change." Yet, knowing it and effectively adopting it are two different things.

We are habitual beings. In fact, scientists estimate that 95 percent of our behaviors are based on habit.[1] In other words, only 5 percent of what we do is based on conscious choice. Not only are we habitual, but we're also neurologically programmed to prefer that things stay the same. Familiarity provides us with a greater sense of psychological safety.

When things do change or become less certain, it's unsettling. We feel like we're out of control. The inability to accept the reality that everything changes is one of the main reasons we create pain and suffering for ourselves. Mindfulness training can be a powerful change management tool. It can help you rewire your brain to be more comfortable with change.

Learning to embrace the reality of constant change is a powerful thing. When we experience a great day at work—or a challenging day—without expecting that the next day will be the same, we become much more resilient in the face of change. Building greater acceptance of the reality of constant change is a foundation for more balance, less stress, better health, and ultimately more peace of mind.

In most, if not all, work environments, change is constant—processes change, systems change, people change, and so on. This is becoming increasingly true as Moore's Law, and the technological growth it charts, begins to touch more and more industries. The extent to which we're able to manage these changes is critical to both our well-being and our ability to realize our potential.

This technique focuses on how mindfulness can help you manage the changes that are imposed externally and outside of your control. We'll look at why we as humans resist change, the power of embracing resistance, and a step-by-step formula for mentally managing change.

Let's start by exploring our automatic response to change: resistance.

Understanding Resistance

To understand the nature of resistance, we first need to know more about our subconscious mind. Constantly scanning the environment, our subconscious mind takes in data from all our senses, directing our behavior without our conscious awareness. The subconscious is driven by self-preservation. If our subconscious mind perceives something in our environment as a threat, we're compelled to act. If it weren't for this process, we might not be alive. At least, our ancestors would have had a smaller chance of surviving.

Today, the challenge results from our subconscious responding to a restructuring at work in much the same way as we would have to an oncoming woolly mammoth. It's a survival instinct.

Hardwired to value certainty, our natural response is to resist uncertainty in our environment. In fact, it would be strange if we didn't experience some resistance to change. Since we're habitual beings, doing anything differently takes effort. Even if the change is something we want, it requires effort to overcome both our neurological impulse to keep things the same as well as our ingrained habitual patterns.

The *Star Trek* television franchise coined the phrase, "Resistance is futile." Since resisting change is completely natural, the expression should more accurately be "Resisting resistance is futile." When we try to resist resistance, we only generate more of it. We create an inner struggle that often leads to anger, frustration, stress, and anxiety. Resisting resistance doesn't help us move forward; instead, it negatively impacts both our health and well-being.

The key to managing resistance and thereby better managing change is to face it and embrace it.

Embracing resistance is not only healthier, but it can also be instructive, enabling us to both accept change and potentially enhance processes and outcomes.

Embracing Resistance

During a major reorganization, Helle, a middle manager in a large European-based global consumer goods manufacturer, shared her experience with the application of mindfulness to managing change. She was asked to lead a change within her unit that she knew was going to be unpopular. She did her best to put the best light on the change, but it was a tough message for her to deliver and for her team to hear.

After the session, one of her staff came into her office and asked to speak with her about the proposed change. They had recently participated in a workshop together on managing change with mindfulness. She took a couple of mindful breaths to ensure that she was able to maintain a relatively open mind and not allow her threat response to be triggered, and invited him in.

He was very calm, which also helped her listen attentively. He said that he had taken a bit of time to absorb the message and recognized some of his resistance was normal. He also felt he had identified some gaps in the proposed rollout that, if addressed, could make things easier for everyone.

Helle was open to hearing his ideas.

Together, they came up with a significantly better plan.

She thanked him, and they shared how pleased they were with their interaction and talked about how applying the principles they had explored in the workshop made the change process much easier.

The mindful approach to managing change outside of your control is to be aware of it, to accept it, and to learn from it. By observing your own resistance neutrally, you can create mental space from it. You stay one second ahead of your reaction—which can be the difference between automatically reacting to a perceived threat or deliberately responding in a constructive way (see Figure T8.1).

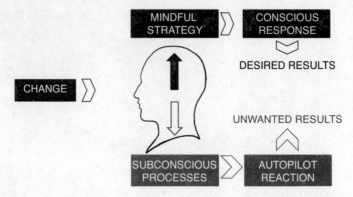

Figure T8.1 Managing change mindfully.

For Helle, this meant taking a deep breath when confronted. For her staff member, it meant staying calm and recognizing his initial resistance was natural.

Of course there's a significant difference between acknowledging and observing resistance and being overcome by the negative emotions it evokes. Once you step back from the experience of resistance, it no longer has the same ability to cloud your mind and sap your energy.

Once you're able to observe your resistance, see whether there's anything you can learn from it. Are you resisting simply because of your natural preference for familiarity? Or are you resisting because something legitimately doesn't make sense? Seeking to understand the underlying driver of your resistance can be insightful.

With clarity of mind and a greater understanding of your resistance, you can more mindfully respond. You can choose to accept the change and let go of your resistance, enabling you to move forward. Or you can choose to mindfully resist the change with focus and awareness.

Although change is constant, managing change isn't easy. To change our behavior, we need two things: motivation and support (see Figure T8.2).

Optimizing the Change Management Process

Like change, motivation can come from both external and internal sources. When change is motivated purely by external sources—by force, with no internal acceptance, for example—people may change their behaviors, but

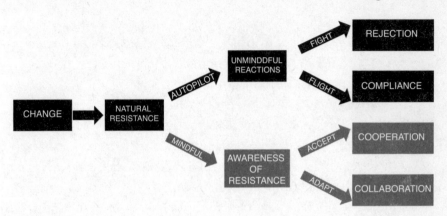

Figure T8.2 The two paths of resistance.

most likely they'll also be resistant and resentful. There may be outward compliance, but it will be given begrudgingly and unsustainably. Given the opportunity to revert to old behaviors, most people will.

However, if an externally motivated change becomes internally accepted, the potential for sustainable change is far greater. This is the power of mindfulness in the change management process.

With mindfulness, individuals can face and accept their own resistance to change. They can make a mindful choice either to embrace the change or mindfully resist it. As we saw in our example with Helle and her coworker, mindful resistance can even enhance the change process.

Ultimately, if we allow ourselves to be driven largely by our unconscious and automatic resistance to change, the results are unnecessary suffering and suboptimal outcomes. If we can apply mindfulness to the change process, however, we can face and embrace our resistance, optimizing outcomes for ourselves and others. Through mindfulness training, we can cultivate both the motivation to move forward and the ability to realize desired results. Here are the five steps for managing change with mindfulness.

Steps for Mindful Change Management

1. Awareness of the change —The first step is simply to recognize that things are changing. Gain as much information as possible regarding the change and what it might entail. Ideally,

this process is done with a mind that accepts the reality of constant change, enabling curiosity, rather than fear, to be the driver behind the investigative process.

2. Awareness of resistance—The second step is to be aware of any resistance to the change. If you think you don't have any resistance, think again. It's natural for us to resist change; there's nothing wrong with resistance. Resistance can be very instructive and can help us gain insight into how to better manage the change. When you become aware of any resistance, don't try to run from it or resist it.

3. Observation of resistance—The third step is to observe the resistance. Seek to understand where it comes from and what might be underlying it. See if there's anything you can learn from it that might inform or enhance the change management process.

4. Mindfully choose your response—With a solid understanding of the change and your resistance to it, you can choose a response. This may mean you choose to fully embrace the change and let go of any resistance. It may also mean you choose to try to skillfully influence the change process by mindfully presenting other alternatives. It may mean you choose not to accept the change because you realize it's not in your best interest. Regardless of your choice, make the decision with a calm, clear mind.

5. Act—The final step is to take action in accordance with your choices. This is where you move forward. Although this step will help you better manage the change process, that doesn't mean it will be easy! It's helpful to acknowledge that it will be difficult to change habitual patterns. You'll likely have ongoing spikes of resistance and setbacks in the process. During this step, it's important to both identify and accept the support you need to manage the change. This could be attending training, being coached, or practicing mindfulness. The gift of mindfulness is that you can continue to apply it as you're going through the change process, making the transition easier and more successful.

The only constant is change. And the only way we grow is by adapting and embracing change. When we resist change without mindfulness, we create unnecessary suffering for ourselves and others. When we embrace change with mindfulness, we're able to take actions in the interest of improving our health, happiness, and realizing our potential. When we resist mindfully and manage change with mindfulness, we move forward, we learn, we develop, we maintain balance, and we optimize outcomes for both ourselves and others.

Next we will explore the potential to enhance mental energy with mindfulness.

Tips and Reflections for Managing Change

- Change is constant. So is our resistance to change. We're habitual beings and don't like change, especially when it's externally imposed.
- Understanding our resistance enables us to separate habitual resistance versus legitimate concerns. This provides us with the opportunity for acceptance and/or a skillful response.
- Being mindful of our resistance and skillful in our response is a solid recipe for successful change, enabling us to work toward greater cooperation and collaboration.
- Consider any changes you're currently facing at work or at home. How could applying more mindfulness be of benefit to yourself or others?

Mental Energy

Aworking day is like a long race. Like a marathon runner, you have to have enough physical and mental energy to make it to the finish line. While most of us are aware of three sources of energy—sufficient sleep, good nutrition, and physical exercise—a fourth source, the mind's own use and maintenance of energy, is often overlooked.

The next three techniques, explore ways mindfulness can help you sleep better, eat more appropriately, and leverage physical activity. But this technique introduces one of the best ways to enhance energy by managing your mind. Let's start by looking at how you thoughts impact your energy and how being mindful can help you conserve energy.

Thoughts, Thought Spirals, and Energy

Some animals hibernate to make sure their physiological energy lasts through the winter. Hibernation reduces the body's metabolism, allowing animals to subsist on little or nothing for extended periods of time.

Now imagine if you could conserve your energy use in a similar way so your energy lasted all day and you had more energy precisely when you needed it. It turns out, you can. And you don't need to sleep through the winter months to do it. Mindfulness training is actually a bit like hibernation.

In one study of the effects of mindfulness on energy consumption, John Ding-E Young and Eugene Taylor asked test subjects to sit still and focus on their breathing.[1] While the subjects sat, researchers monitored and measured changes in their physiology. Over the course of a few minutes, the researchers noticed changes similar to animal hibernation, such as lower oxygen consumption and slower breathing. The test subjects' bodies entered into a state resembling deep sleep, despite the fact their minds were very much aware and focused. If these kinds of changes occur over the course of a few minutes, imagine the kind of energy you can save with extended practice.

According to research, without regular training, our mind has a tendency to wander aimlessly almost half of our waking hours.[2] When our minds wander—when we're not focused—some of our energy dissipates. And it's not just the fact that a wandering mind uses up valuable mental energy. Where our mind goes when it wanders can also play a role. When we're worried or anxious, or when we're filled with frustration or anger, it can be easy for our thoughts to spiral out of control.

For many people, negative emotions can quickly and easily drain mental energy. But positive thought spirals can be equally draining. We've all had the experience of eagerly anticipating an event. It can be hard to contain our excitement, to stop thinking about the target of our anticipation. Even though a thought spiral might be about something positive, it's a spiral nonetheless. And all of that thinking uses up glucose and oxygen, the fuel for our brain. Our thoughts have an incredibly powerful impact on our mental health and well-being. Positive or negative thinking can be mentally and physically exhausting.

With mindfulness training, you strengthen your focus and awareness— giving you the time and ability to choose the objects of your attention, as well as helping you best conserve mental energy.

Enhancing Mental Energy

When it comes to conserving mental energy, mindfulness can help in four key ways: being present, maintaining balance, making choices, and leveraging cycles.

Four Mindful Ways to Conserve Mental Energy

1. **Being Present**—Being present in the here and now is a simple and easy way to conserve mental resources. When we allow our mind to wander aimlessly, it's using up valuable energy that could be better used in other pursuits. Making a choice to be present in the moment optimizes energy usage.

2. **Maintaining Balance**—Awareness of negative or positive thought spirals allows us to leverage balance. Being aware of the mind's tendency to succumb to attraction or aversion—to run toward things we want or away from things we don't want—is powerful. By maintaining balance in our mind, we can further conserve energy.

3. **Making Choices**—To manage mental energy we must be aware of the impact our experiences have on our energy. Such awareness can help us make conscious choices about how we spend our time. Avoid multitasking. Follow the first rule of mental effectiveness and choose a task and stick with it. Notice the impact that not jumping back and forth between tasks can have on your energy.

4. **Leveraging Cycles**—Our mental energy naturally ebbs and flows throughout the day, in cycles that have a lot to do with our sleep, nutrition, and level of physical activity. We simply are not always at peak mental performance. For most people, energy levels are higher first thing in the morning, after a good night's rest. Those energy levels tend to decrease during the day, with a low point after lunch, before increasing again later in the afternoon. Being mindful of our how our energy levels fluctuate enables us to be strategic about what we do and when. For example, if you need to do a complicated analysis or solve a complex problem, it's best done when our energy levels are higher. Tasks such as sorting through our e-mail may be performed effectively even with a lower level of energy.

Mindfulness training can also help you conserve mental energy in a much more foundational way. The better we're able to focus and the more aware we become of our thought processes, the more likely we are to spot predicaments of our own creation.

Linda was a manager with a large research institute in America. After the workshop on Energy Management, she noticed the negative impact watching television had on her energy.

At the end of a long workday, she enjoyed the idea of sitting in front of the television as a form of relaxation. But what she noticed was that in general, the actual experience of watching television was more of a drain than a gain on her energy. She decided to test the impact of turning the television off during supper and the family then going for a walk or being outside for a while.

Although there was some initial resistance from family members, and some longstanding powerful habits had to be confronted, after a few days Linda was surprised how much more energy she had in the evening. Further, she was amazed how it improved the quality of the family time.

Linda was so inspired by these results that she also started to map her energy throughout the day and seek to match activities with her energy cycles. For example, she realized she was at peak energy early in the morning and so rearranged her schedule to get to work early to read scientific documents and create reports. It also became apparent she hit an energy lull around 10:30 a.m. and she decided this was a good time to go through her inbox.

Most of us are no different. In the face of uncertainty, stress, and everyday worries, our mind spirals toward the worst possible outcome. Thankfully, with mindfulness training, we can learn to spot the seeds of these energy-sapping "problems" early on, helping us decide where to spend our mental energy and where to save it. By being attentive to how we use, conserve, and maintain all four sources of energy—sleep, nutrition, exercise, and our mind—we can have more energy to excel in a high-paced work setting, be less stressed, and have a greater peace of mind.

The next technique presents tips on how to enhance sleep with mindfulness.

Tips and Reflections for Managing Mental Energy

- Our thoughts are not just air. What we think about and how much time we spend thinking about issues—both positive and negative—have a tremendous impact on our mental energy.
- Take time over the next week to notice how thoughts impact your energy, as well as how your energy naturally ebbs and flows throughout the day.
- Consider ways that you can enhance your mental energy by being present, maintaining balance, making choices, and leveraging daily energy cycles.

TECHNIQUE #10

Enhancing Sleep

Ah, sleep.

Wonderful, glorious sleep.

Think back to a time when you had two or three consecutive nights of really good sleep. Hopefully, it wasn't *too* long ago. Maybe you were on vacation. Or maybe you were just at home for a long weekend. How did it impact your mood? Your creativity and energy? How did it affect your focus, clarity, and performance? If I had to wager, I'd guess your focus was sharp, your clarity crystalline, and your performance solid.

Now, think about the last time you had too little sleep. Maybe you had a big presentation to prepare at the eleventh hour and had to work late. Or maybe you just weren't feeling well and couldn't get to sleep, but still had to get up to go to work in the morning. Most people tend to agree that getting too little sleep can seriously impact our performance and well-being on many levels—and there is a growing body of research to back it up.

A number of scientific studies have shown sleep deprivation to be one of the issues underlying a long list of mental and physical disorders.[1] Even light sleep deprivation has been proven to negatively impact logical reasoning, executive function, attention, and mood. More severe sleep deprivation can lead to depression, anxiety, paranoia, and even coma or death (see Figure T10.1). While humans can survive quite a few weeks without food and up to a week without water, they can only go four days without sleep.

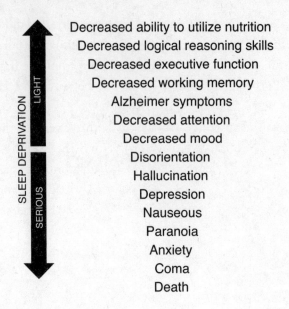

Figure T10.1 The impact of sleep deprivation.

Yet despite the undeniable importance of sleep for our overall health and well-being, it's often the first thing many of us compromise. As a result of our busy lifestyles, sleep is regularly pushed toward the bottom of our list of priorities. After all, there are only so many hours in a day. But even light sleep deprivation can result in reduced performance and poor health.

Fortunately, research has shown regular mindfulness training improves the ability to fall asleep and sleep quality significantly.[2] Whether you are a person who only needs a little sleep or someone who needs a lot, enhancing how quickly and effectively you sleep can enhance performance and make better use of your time.

This techniques looks at ways to use mindfulness while falling asleep and waking up. To begin, here are three simple guidelines that can help you sleep better.

Guideline #1: Catch the Melatonin Wave

A complex mixture of neurochemicals in your brain and body—the most important of which is melatonin—determines the quality of your sleep. Melatonin, when released from the pineal gland deep inside your brain, makes you relaxed, drowsy, and ultimately fall asleep.[3] It's a great, organic, and natural drug. If you learn to notice it and go with its flow, you'll enjoy falling asleep and have better quality sleep during the night.

The release of melatonin has its own rhythm over a 24-hour period: from very low in the daytime, rising through the evening, and peaking around 2 a.m.[4] By the next morning, melatonin is again down to its low daytime level. As Figure T10.2 shows, the peaks and valleys of your melatonin levels form a beautiful wave over the course of the day and night.

And the wave of melatonin is more than just something nice to look at on a graph. In fact, it's a wave you can catch for better sleep. How? It's a lot like surfing: to successfully ride a wave, you need to catch it in its earlier stages. From then on, let it carry you through a good night of sleep, to the shores of morning.

The key to catching the melatonin wave is to be mindful: have awareness of the natural drowsiness and relaxation that occur toward the end of the evening and maintain that awareness as you prepare for bed. If you try to keep yourself awake—which is very possible, and many of us often do—you'll miss the ideal opportunity to catch the melatonin wave. Like catching a wave that has already broken, it might

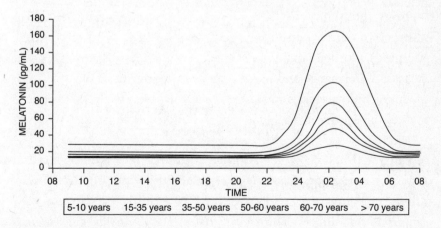

Figure T10.2   Daily melatonin levels.

push you toward the shore, but it probably won't be the most pleasant or effective experience.

Besides getting in sync with your own cycle of melatonin, another simple way to get a better night's sleep is to reduce or eliminate screen time before going to bed.

Guideline #2: TURN off All Screens
60 Minutes before Sleep

If you're reading this chapter on a screen in bed, please stop.

Your smartphone, your tablet, your laptop, your television, and any other screen you may have all stand in the way of you catching the melatonin wave. How? Each of those screens emits high levels of blue light rays. That blue light suppresses your pineal gland, and, in turn, the production of melatonin.[5] Where the sun was once the only light setting your neurological clock, artificial light threatens to throw that natural rhythm out of whack.

To put it simply, screen light kills your sleep. It's almost like your brain reads the blue light as if the sun is still up, when in reality the sun has probably been down for hours and you should be sleeping.

To avoid the circadian confusion blue light exposure can cause, turn off all screens one hour before you go to sleep. All of them. It might sound difficult to some, but it works. The impact it has on sleep quality—and therefore mental and physical performance—speaks for itself.

Of course, quitting any habit cold turkey can be difficult. To help facilitate the change, try replacing your hour of pre-bed screen time with 60 minutes of perceptual activities.

Guideline #3: Perceptual Activities
60 Minutes before Sleep

Too much thinking is yet another enemy of late evening natural relaxation and drowsiness. *Conceptual* activities like intense conversations, replying to e-mails, working, or reading can arouse your attention and suppress your natural sleepiness. However, *perceptual* activities like doing the dishes, going for a walk, or listening to music can help you catch the wave of melatonin as it rises. Simply being mindful of melatonin's changing levels can help you better go with its flow.

Before you say, "That's impossible," think about your evening routine. Even if you typically work on your computer right up until bedtime, there's no concrete reason that always needs to be the case.

Melissa, an employee in the Australia Federal Government, viewed these guidelines as utterly impossible when they were first presented to her. She was used to working most nights on her computer or iPad or phone until she went to bed. However, she was inspired by the scientific evidence and motivated to find a way of making it work.

After discussion with other program participants, she decided to restructure her evening activities. Instead of doing the dishes and other practical activities just after dinner, she left that for the last hour before sleep, instead of screen activities. This allowed her to still do some work in the evening, while leaving the last hour before sleep for perceptual activities with no screens and an opportunity to be aware of the melatonin wave.

Just a small adjustment to your evening routine can go a long way toward enabling you to prepare for bed with a calmer mind that's more in tune with the natural rhythms of your body. So save the dishes, walking the dog, or taking out the trash for the last hour of the evening. Sometimes procrastination can pay off.

Then, as you let go of the final minutes of the day, consider the following strategies for falling asleep mindfully.

Falling Asleep Mindfully

What does your bedroom look like? Is it clean or cluttered? A calm space or a chaotic one? The more you can do to turn your bedroom into a sleep sanctuary, the better off you'll be. Allow your bedroom to be a nonconceptual place. Check your screens, serious conversations, and thinking at the door.

Beyond making your bedroom into a shrine to sleep, these steps will help you calm your mind and best catch the melatonin wave.

Falling Asleep Mindfully

- Before you lie down, sit on the edge of your bed, close your eyes, and do one or more minutes of mindfulness training, as outlined in Part III of this book. Allow any thoughts of unresolved business to arise, and then let them go. Center yourself with your breath. Allow your body to relax. Allow your mind to relax. Breathe and let go.
- Lie down on your back. Maintain a gentle awareness of your breath while relaxing your body and mind deeper with each exhalation. Do not force your attention on your breath as that will arouse wakefulness. Simply relax and let go.
- After a short while, you'll experience your awareness fading away. When this happens, roll onto your right side; let go of any remaining awareness; and allow yourself to fade into sleep.

If you have a tendency to wake up in the middle of the night, repeat the two last steps. If you wake up agitated—maybe because you have an important meeting coming up and need your rest—find the courage to face the agitation.

Ultimately, the root of your sleep disturbances is in your mind, whether stress, uncertainty, or anything else. And the problem can only be solved at its source.

I've explained how mindfulness can help you get to sleep and enjoy good quality sleep time, but mindfulness can also help you wake up better prepared to face the day.

Waking Up Mindfully

Ever wake up grouchy or anxious?

It turns out there's some science behind the common symptoms of getting up on the wrong side of the bed. In fact, researchers have found that many people have the highest level of the stress hormone cortisol in their blood in the minutes after they wake up.[6] This early rush of cortisol is triggered when we immediately start thinking about everything we have to do in the coming day.

Compounding the problem, once cortisol has been released into our bloodstreams, our bodies take a long time and a lot of energy to bring the levels back down (see Figure T10.3). When we first wake up, the mind's natural defense mechanisms have not yet been activated. The result is a stressful start to the day and a massive loss of energy.

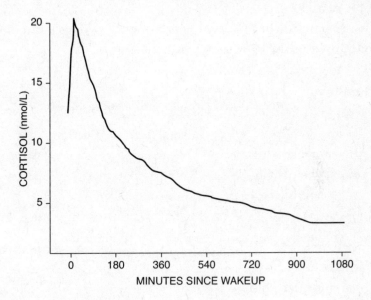

Figure T10.3 Daily cortisol levels.

Allowing yourself to wake up peacefully can save you a lot of unnecessarily wasted energy for the rest of the day. Mindfulness can help you minimize—or entirely avoid—the a.m. cortisol rush. It can be the difference between starting the day one second ahead or already falling behind before you've even had a chance to get out of bed. To wake mindfully, follow these steps.

Waking Mindfully

- As you wake, be determined not to start thinking. Just be. Notice your body. Notice your mind. But do not engage in the thoughts trying to arise. Sit up, at the edge of your bed, and do two minutes of mindfulness training (see Part III). Focus on your breath and let go of any thoughts.

When you set yourself up for the best possible sleep, you'll have better focus and clarity. And ultimately, you'll have better results in your day. While getting a great night's sleep may require a few changes to entrenched habits and a few minutes of training before and after sleep, the benefits are invaluable. Give it a try for a month and see what it does for you.

The next technique looks at some of the ways you can further enhance your energy by what, when, and how you eat.

Tips and Reflections for Enhancing Sleep

- Take a moment to reflect on your own sleep patterns. Do you get enough sleep at night? When you go to bed, are you able to get to sleep quickly? What's your experience with the quality of your sleep? Is there room for improvement?
- Try one or two of the sleep guidelines provided for one week. Then note any impact on your energy and effectiveness.

TECHNIQUE #11

Eating and Energy

As the saying goes, "You are what you eat."

The food you eat is closely linked to your ability to focus, find clarity, and be productive. In addition, eating the right things, at the right time, in the right amounts, is one sure way of enhancing your energy levels.

Many of us lead hectic lives. When we're under pressure and caught up in the never-ending stream of routine and responsibilities, we sometimes fall into unfortunate eating habits. This means eating right can be a daily challenge, particularly in a world where fast food is so readily available.

While discipline may get you part of the way toward eating well, eating what you like with mindfulness is a gentler—and perhaps even more pleasant—way to get the energy you need while simultaneously enhancing health and well-being.

This technique explains how our brain tricks us into developing unhealthy eating habits. It also covers the ways mindfulness can help foster healthier habits of eating what we need, rather than what we crave. To get the most out of mindful eating, there are three basic guidelines: letting your stomach do the eating, avoiding the blood sugar roller coaster, and taking the mindful minute.

Guideline # 1: Let Your Stomach Do the Eating

Our eyes are hungrier than our stomachs.

This isn't just an idiom but also a conclusion reached by researchers from Cornell University.[1] During one study, participants went, one at a time, into a room containing a chair, a table, a bowl of soup, and a spoon. They were then asked to eat the soup.

Unbeknown to half of the individuals, while they were eating, the bowl was being refilled by a hose attached to the bottom of the bowl. It was quite literally a bottomless bowl of soup.

Amazingly, participants who ate from the unlimited soup bowl consumed 73 percent more than those who ate from a regular bowl. When asked if they were full, a common response was "how can I be full? I still have half a bowl left."

Why do we sometimes eat more than we need? Research suggests that when we're too focused on finishing what's in front of us, we lose the mindful awareness that our stomach might already be full. We go on autopilot, eating out of habit rather than necessity.

A simple mindful tip for eating is to let your stomach do the eating. There's no need to finish everything in front of you right this second. Refrigerators and take-away cartons are great modern innovations— and tomorrow is another day. When you're full, or even better, before you are full, stop eating. Staying mindfully aware of when you have had enough will not only help you eat better, but feel better too.

But what about those mid-afternoon hankerings for a quick fix of junk food? It turns out, when it comes to sugary snacks, your mind may have a mind of its own.

Guideline # 2: Avoid the Blood Sugar Rollercoaster

In a study at California State University, two groups of participants were asked to manage their energy, tiredness, and tension.[2] The first group was asked to manage by taking a brisk ten-minute walk. The second group, by eating a candy bar.

The walkers reported a significant increase in energy and a significant decrease in both tiredness and tension. The sugar snackers, on the other hand, reported higher energy initially, followed by low energy, tiredness, and increased tension.

Many of us, seeking a quick antidote to feeling sleepy, ride the blood sugar rollercoaster during the afternoon hours. An hour or two after lunch, we hit the afternoon slump—a fatigue our brains mistakes for a lack of blood glucose. A natural and automatic reaction is to grab a snack, a cup of coffee, or an energy drink to quickly raise our energy levels. But a snack—and a sugary one in particular—can raise blood sugar levels too high, leading to mood swings, brain fog, and stress.

After a short while, blood sugar levels plummet. A sense of panic results due to the stress, cortisol, and adrenaline released when fatigue and brain fog set in. Then we're right back where we started, at the bottom of the roller coaster, with our brains craving another fix of fast energy. To get a better picture of this cycle, take a look at Figure T11.1.

Whether you find yourself at the top or bottom of the ride, your focus and clarity both suffer. Neither the body nor the brain really needs the extra sugar, no matter how much it might feel like it. Still, when we're not aware of our cravings, or of the natural ebb and flow of our own energy levels throughout the day, we can be easily tricked into going for a ride.

How do we hop off the blood sugar roller coaster?

Simple. Take a mindful minute.

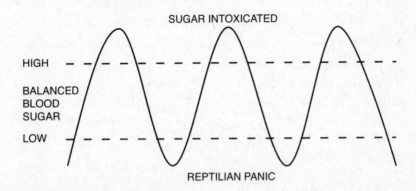

Figure T11.1   The blood sugar roller coaster.

Guideline # 3: The Mindful Minute

The mindful minute—as shown in Figure T11.2—is a self-directed way to avoid undesired and mindless snacking.

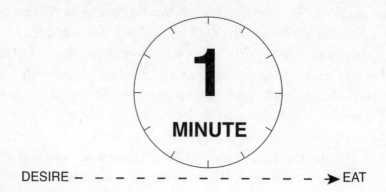

Figure T11.2 The mindful minute.

Over time, allowing yourself a mindful minute before immediately snacking can mitigate the general craving that comes with natural tiredness. The guidelines are simple.

Take a Mindful Minute

- Next time you feel desire for food, pause.
- Allow yourself to mindfully observe the experience of desire. Allow the experience to be present, without engaging and giving in to it. This is not meant to impart strict discipline and impulse control, merely a moment of mindfulness before you eat.
- Ask yourself, what does it feel like? Where do you experience the feeling, in your stomach or elsewhere? Is the experience changing or does it stay the same?
- If after the minute, you're feeling the same desire, you may actually be hungry. In that case, eat.
- If there's little or no desire left, you weren't actually hungry. Your brain tried to trick you. But you were smarter, and dismantled the desire by simply allowing it to rise without engaging in it.

In the general busyness of everyday, it's easy to default to unhealthy eating patterns. Andrew, for example, worked long hours in the Singapore office of a large European Bank. While he loved coming home with takeout from his favorite Dim Sum restaurant—and sometimes a candy bar for good measure—he didn't love what was happening to his waistline as a result.

Initially, he laughed at the suggestion of simply waiting a minute before eating things he probably shouldn't. But then, over time, it got easier. He began observing his cravings rather than immediately acting upon them. Eventually, his cravings weakened to the point where he could resist them.

Andrew still enjoys the occasional candy bar but as a conscious choice versus an autopilot behavior. He has also noticed that when he does indulge, he eats much less and enjoys it much more.

While it's important to stop yourself from eating on autopilot, it's just as important to eat the right amounts of the right foods at the right time. In fact, the three mindful eating guidelines could be condensed into just one master guideline: eat what you eat, but do it mindfully.

The Essence of Mindful Eating

There are thousands of diet plans, each of which claims to be more effective than the last. Each has stringent rules about what you can and can't eat. Some even necessitate drastic changes to your lifestyle. Most, at the very least, require restraint, discipline, and impulse control. While that can all be useful, the mindful approach can increase your chances of success. How? By getting to the root cause of any undesired eating habits: the mind.

When you're mindful of your food, awareness tells you when you have had enough. You tend to eat less. You also tend to enjoy food more, because you actually pay attention to it. In a gentle way, you dismantle the brain's shortcomings, allowing you to eat the foods you need to best sustain mental and physical performance. Now, enjoy your next meal, with greater awareness of the difference between your eyes and your stomach: between automatic cravings and actual hunger.

The next technique examines how mindfulness can further enhance energy through physical activity.

Tips and Reflections for Eating and Energy

- With a nonjudgmental and curious mind, reflect on your eating habits, particularly with respect to how what you eat impacts your energy and effectiveness.
- Consider these questions: What do you eat that helps you be more present, focused, and clear minded? At what times do you generally need to eat and what effect does this have on your state of mind? Is your general intake of food too big, too small, or balanced in relation to your physical and mental performance?
- Try applying one or two of the mindful nutrition guidelines for a week. See if you notice any impact on your energy levels.

TECHNIQUE #12

Activity and Energy

Think about the last time you went for a walk or had a really great workout. How did you feel? Odds are, you probably felt good.

Your mind and body are connected on a deep level. Energies flow freely between the two. When you have positive physical experiences, your mind smiles.

In this way, caring for the body is just as impactful as caring for the mind. Getting good and sufficient sleep, eating properly, and being physically active are all foundations for both performance and well-being.

You don't have to run a marathon or climb mountains or do 50 push-ups to achieve results. Any type of physical activity has a strong positive influence on your body and your brain. From swimming to gardening to taking the stairs instead of the elevator, anything that gets you up and moving is a lift to your mind, health and well-being.

In your everyday work life, take advantage of any opportunity for physical activity. For example, ride your bike to work or walk the ten blocks instead of taking the bus. Just ten minutes of brisk walking will make you feel more energized and less tired. Besides, how many times a day do you already walk from your office to a meeting or to the restroom or to the parking lot? Each one of those small walks is a terrific opportunity to give your body a little extra attention.

As with mindfulness, there is a tremendous amount of evidence showing the benefits of keeping your body in good shape. This technique examines how mindfulness training and physical activity make a powerful recipe for better health, increased mental focus, and greater clarity. Let's start by looking at the importance of focus in physical activity.

Maintain Your Focus

Maintaining a clear focus while undertaking physical activity transforms a workout into a semi-mindfulness session and will improve your experience. Next time you exercise, be aware of what your thoughts do to your energy level. What happens when you think positive thoughts? Neutral thoughts? Negative thoughts? What do mental distractions do to your energy levels?

Thoughts and distractions drain energy to different extents. Negative thoughts are the worst, but even positive thoughts have a downside. A calm, clear, focused mind doesn't drain your energy while being physical and allows you to perform longer. Try it for yourself and see how it works for you. Then consider the connection between relaxation and performance.

Relaxation—The Absence of Unnecessary Effort

As in mindfulness training, relaxation is essential for physical activity to be effective. While it may seem contradictory to equate relaxation and physical activity, it's not. To be clear, I'm not saying you should ride a recumbent bicycle or lift weights while reclining on the couch. That's not relaxation in its truest sense. Relaxation is the absence of unnecessary effort. Relaxation is the path of least resistance.

Take free divers, for example. Free divers swim deep under water for long periods of time without the benefit of oxygen tanks. Once a world record holder, Stig Åvall Severinsen held his breath under water for 20 minutes and 10 seconds. By working with his breathing and focus, he saved energy, decreased his oxygen expenditure, and increased his performance. When we're focused, we use less energy and become more effective and efficient.

A relaxed body—one absent of unnecessary tension—has greater endurance and generally feels more pleasant. As you train, occasionally scan your body for signs of unnecessary effort or tension. Then relax. The more relaxed you are, the more you can do and the more you'll enjoy it.

While relaxation is also important for the mind to avoid thinking and distraction, the mind needs an object of focus. You need to have an anchor—and that anchor is usually your breath. While breathing is a great anchor while you're sitting still, it's equally powerful during physical activity. But breath alone may not be enough. Instead, it can be more effective to synchronize your breath with the natural rhythm of your physical activity.

Focus on the Rhythm

When we do physical exercise, there's a natural rhythm to our movements, our breathing, and other bodily functions. Use that natural rhythm to strengthen your focus. When you run or walk, synchronize your steps with your breath. Take a certain number of steps for each inhalation and each exhalation. This way, you can easily maintain a focused and steady rhythm for long periods. It's often easier than just focusing on your breathing.

Focus and rhythm can be a big help, especially if you feel poorly or experience pain. Most unpleasantness comes from our thoughts. Thoughts come from physical sensations or other distractions. Your focus creates your reality. Focus on unpleasantness, and your reality will be unpleasant. Instead, focus on your breathing and rhythm—and experience one moment at a time.

As distractions appear, don't try to suppress them. Simply take one moment after the other: one step after the other. Inhale and exhale. Don't think about how much time you have left. Stay in the moment. With relaxed focus, any unpleasantness or pain will diminish.

Any kind of physical activity will help you gain better focus and clarity—and by applying the principles of mindfulness you can enhance your performance. By helping you maintain focus, relaxation, and rhythm, mindfulness increases the enjoyment and effectiveness of activity.

The next technique will explore a simple, yet powerful way to enhance productivity and energy throughout the day by taking regular performance breaks.

Tips and Reflections for Activity and Energy

- The mind and body are connected. If we want to have a healthy, engaged, active mind, we need to have a healthy, engaged, active body.
- Reflect on your level of activity during a week. Do you take advantage of opportunities to increase activity? Do you get enough exercise through planned activities?
- Consider ways you can use focus, relaxation, and rhythm to enhance physical activity—and use physical activity to enhance your focus, relaxation, and rhythm.

TECHNIQUE #13

Performance Breaks

Many of us are so busy, we forget to take a break. Often, the only break we do take is for lunch. And even that "break" is often only the five minutes it takes to grab food and bring it back to our desk. Take a moment to consider two quick questions: How often do you take breaks during a workday? What keeps you from taking more breaks?

Interestingly enough, quite often the main barrier between ourselves and taking breaks is not our organization or its management. In fact, most organizations and managers recognize the value of breaks—many even encourage them.

It turns out the greatest enemy of breaks is most often ourselves.

But breaks are actually quite important—for our happiness, our health, our overall well-being, and our performance.

And the great thing is, good quality performance enhancing breaks can take less than a minute.

Mindful Performance Breaks

A day without breaks is for the mind what running a marathon without water is for the body: unnecessarily exhausting. Taking mindful performance breaks is both a time-efficient and nourishing way of maintaining focus and clarity.

A mindful performance break is basically a very brief mindfulness training session. And by brief, I mean about 45 seconds. To take mindful performance breaks, try this, once every hour during work.

Taking Mindful Performance Breaks

- Let go of your activities. You don't need to go anywhere special. Close your eyes or keep them open, whichever you prefer.
- Direct your full attention to your breath. For three breath cycles do the following:
- Breathe in while noticing your breath; breathe out while relaxing your shoulders, neck, and arms.
- Breathe in while focusing fully on your inhale; breathe out while focusing on the exhale.
- Breathe in while enhancing the clarity of your attention; breathe out while maintaining clarity.
- Let go of the exercise. Return to your work with renewed relaxation, focus, and clarity.

A mindful performance break is about giving your mind a chance to recover from the constant *conceptual* activity work requires. The conceptual state is a "doing" state—concerned mostly with accomplishing tasks as quickly and efficiently as possible. A mindful performance break, however, pushes your mind into more of a "being" or *perpetual* state. This state gives our mind a chance to simply be.

Conceptual and perceptual states are the two fundamental modes of our brain (see Figure T13.1). The conceptual mind is what we use to plan, problem solve, and think. Most of us are in a conceptual state most of the time. The perceptual state, on the other hand, is one of observation.

The benefits of allowing our brains small, regular breaks from conceptual activity are numerous: our brain is re-energized, our mind is more focused and clear, our body is more relaxed, and we break the spell of action addiction.

Obviously, you won't always be able to take a performance break every hour. Participants in important meetings often frown on alarms

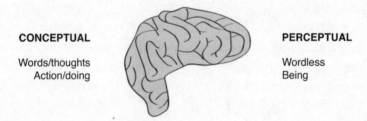

CONCEPTUAL		PERCEPTUAL
Words/thoughts Action/doing		Wordless Being

Figure T13.1 The conceptual and perceptual mind.

going off, as well as participants stepping away mid-meeting to run through breathing exercises. If you have to skip breaks, it's not the end of the world. The more you take them, though, the more rested and effective your mind will be throughout the day.

While mindful breaks are easy to do, they're just as easy to forget. We have made it easy for you to incorporate this break into your daily routine by developing an app for your smartphone or tablet that will give you a reminder once an hour. You can find a link to it our website, www.potentialproject.com, or go directly to the app store on your phone and search The Potential Project.

If hourly breaks don't work for you, there are many other ways to remind yourself to take mindful breaks. Every time your phone rings, try taking a mindful breath before you answer. Or every time you transition between activities—from meeting to e-mail, e-mail to car, car to home—take a short break. Find out what works best for you. Remember, every time you practice mindfulness, you create more neural connections, making it easier and easier to find your focus and clarity whenever you need it. The next technique looks at how to get better use of the often wasted time, traveling to and from work with mindful commuting.

Tips and Reflections for Performance Breaks

- Our minds have two modes of operating: conceptual and perceptual.
- Most of us spend the majority of our days in a conceptual mode—the mode that involves thinking and communicating.

- Performance breaks are about giving your mind a reprieve from thinking. Being in an experiential, perceptual state enhances balance and resilience.
- Consider ways that you can introduce more performance breaks into your workday.
- To make it easier to stay on track, you can find an app that reminds you to break once every hour at www.potentialproject.com or in the iOS or Android app store.

TECHNIQUE #14

Commuting

Eric was a senior manager with a global American technology company based in California. With a large department to manage, he was very busy. For him, mindfulness training was important. When he practiced, it helped him stay focused—and sane.

Even so, as time went on, he found that he practiced less and less frequently.

Despite our best intentions, the real world sometimes has other plans for us. The reality of Eric's everyday schedule—the relentless e-mails, the back-to-back meetings, and a home with three children—made it difficult, if not impossible, to commit to 10 minutes of daily mindfulness practice. For weeks, he struggled to fit those ten minutes into his already packed schedule.

Then it hit him.

Eric had a 40-minute commute. Each morning, and each afternoon, he spent 40 minutes, by himself, in his car.

Eric thought of his commute as a relaxing time. But the more aware he became of how his mind and body worked, the more he realized he wasn't relaxing at all. He was actually multitasking—or at least trying to—during each 40-minute commute. He was making phone calls, searching for music on the radio, or honking at the other drivers who cut him off on the freeway.

It turns out, those supposedly serene commutes were far more stressful than Eric initially thought. So instead of trying to cram all that activity into a moving vehicle, Eric decided to devote some of that time to his daily mindfulness training. He was captive to the traffic anyway: why not make use of it? Not only did this help him arrive at work more focused, but at the end of the day he returned to his family with increased presence and a greater peace of mind.

You've likely arrived at work with your mind still preoccupied by what happened throughout your morning. Or maybe you've arrived home after work, but your mind didn't arrive with you: it was still working away at the office. If you've experienced either of these states, you've been on autopilot. You've been sacrificing your own productivity, effectiveness, and well-being. But most important, you've been missing out on valuable moments in your life.

Commuting with mindfulness is a simple yet profound way to reclaim this time and spend it in a worthwhile way: on cultivating greater focus and clarity.

The "How" of Mindful Commuting

There are a few specific instructions for commuting with mindfulness, depending on how you travel. Whether you're driving, taking the bus, or traveling by plane, harnessing even a portion of these travel hours for mindfulness training can make you more focused and effective. To learn how, consider the following directions for mindful commuting.

Commuting to Enhance Focus and Clarity

- **Passive transport:** When traveling short distances by public transportation, taxi, or any other vehicle someone else is operating, use the first five minutes (or more) and the last five (or more) to practice the ABCD focus training described in Chapter 2. Give your full attention to the experience of breathing, count in cycles, and let go of distractions.
- **Active transport:** If you're traveling by bike, car, motorcycle, or anything else of which you're in control, ease into and out of the ride. For the first five minutes (or more) and the last five (or

more), turn off the radio, and take a break from talking on the phone. Give your full awareness to your hands on the steering wheel, your feet on the pedals, and the traffic around you. In other words, be fully present with the experience of driving, riding, or cycling. Let go of any other thoughts that arise.

- **Longer journeys:** When you travel by train or plane—especially on long flights across several time zones—mindfulness can be a great way to arrive refreshed and restored. Take ten minutes or more once an hour, for as long as the journey lasts, to close your eyes and do mindfulness training as described in Part III of this book. From Europe, I often travel to Asia, Australia, and North America for conferences and meetings. My jet lag is significantly less when I practice mindfulness in the air.

The minutes or hours we use commuting to and from work are valuable. Rather than letting them go to waste on the frustrations of freeway congestion or the illusion of multitasking, use them to develop focus and clarity. Allow yourself to take a well-earned break from your thoughts. Enjoy the experience of driving, riding, or sitting.

Effectively used, commuting time can ensure we arrive at work with clarity and at home with full presence. By separating work and home with a mindful commute, we have the potential to enhance work life balance which is explored further in Technique #16. And this type of balance makes us happier, healthier, and more effective in both settings.

The next technique looks at how mindfulness can help with maintaining emotional balance.

Tips and Reflections for Mindful Commuting

- Consider: Is your current commute relaxing? Or is it really just a stressful time in which you try to juggle calls, the radio, and thoughts of upcoming meetings or errands?
- Mindfully managing the transition to and from work is a terrific way to increase balance and resilience.

- Doing some mindfulness training during your commute can help you arrive at work or at home with more focus and awareness and less stress.
- How much time do you spend getting to and from work? Consider using at least some of that time strategically to train in mindfulness, as outlined in Part III.

TECHNIQUE #15

Emotional Balance

Working in any organization can be challenging. Each day, we make choices and act in ways that often have consequences for other people. While sometimes those consequences are positive, that's not always the case. When our actions result in negative consequences for other people, it's normal for them to respond emotionally—often in ways that are not helpful for the organization or for their own health and well-being.

Emotions are a natural part of being human. Managed skillfully, they're a powerful source of joy and energy. Unsuccessfully managed, however, they can get in the way, becoming a source of frustration, conflict, and regret.

To be clear, emotional balance has nothing to do with suppressing or getting rid of our emotions. Neither is it about giving them power over our lives. In reality, having emotional balance equates to not getting caught up in the natural ups and downs of our emotions. Emotional balance is a state of being aware of our emotions enough to manage them in a way that is gentle, honest, and wise.

Emotional balance comes from having emotional intelligence combined with a trained mind that's able to notice and respond to emotions when they arise. It makes a significant difference in the work environment in terms of how people interact and work together.

This technique examines the basics of maintaining emotional balance. We'll look at the ways emotional balance is important at work and some of the reasons it can be difficult to maintain. Lastly, I'll provide some ways to use mindfulness to maintain emotional balance in the midst of emotional turbulence.

The Basic Reactions to Emotions

Thomas, a department head for a large European manufacturing company, was directed to let go 25 percent of his staff. Telling these people—some of whom he'd worked with for years—that they were out of a job, was one of the worst tasks he could imagine. The stress of these impending conversations kept him up at night, decreased his effectiveness, and compromised his balance and resilience.

Thomas knew what emotions he would feel during the layoff meetings. He knew seeing people he cared for in distress would make him distressed. And the distress would stay with him for hours afterward. In fact, it would be strange if he weren't distressed.

Mirroring others' emotions is normal; it's your mirror neurons at play. More about mirror neurons is presented in the mental strategy of Joy. But in short, when we face someone joyful, mirror neurons in our brains make us experience a similar joy. The same goes for anger, grief, and almost all other emotions.

Thomas's challenge, then, was to handle his emotions professionally. It was to expect to feel grief, regret, and maybe even sadness, all while keeping a calm, clear mind that would allow him to best serve those on the receiving end of the bad news.

Most of us deal with our emotions by either suppressing them or acting them out. The thing about suppressing emotions is that they have to go somewhere. Like pressing down on a balloon, pushing your emotions down only means they will pop up again somewhere else. Additionally, suppressing emotions requires an enormous amount of mental energy—energy that's diverted from our own focus and clarity. Acting out our emotions, whether aggressively or passive aggressively, might feel good in the moment. But if acting out is effective at all, it's only in that moment. In the long run, acting out our emotions usually leads to disappointment, regret, or shame.

Think of emotional suppression and acting out as being on opposite sides of a seesaw (see Figure T15.1). Putting your weight on either end throws off the balance.

Figure T15.1 Mindful emotional balance.

Instead of choosing either of these automatic reactions to emotion, consider a third option. By utilizing mindfulness, you can maintain emotional balance, even in the face of difficult emotions. The following are a few ways to think about and embrace emotions as they arise in work and in life.

Maintaining Emotional Balance

In mindfulness training, we work to develop the mental capacity, the patience, and the courage to endure discomfort. At the same time, we learn to observe our emotions with some neutrality. We put some kind of distance between our emotions and ourselves. Instead of running on autopilot, being absorbed with emotion and caught in its grip, we take a moment to pause. We stay one second ahead of automatic reactions, giving ourselves the time, space, and freedom to make conscious, deliberate choices.

When you've trained these skills for a while, they become easier to apply across situations. To maintain emotional balance, apply these four steps: become aware of the emotion, embrace the emotion, employ patience and balance, and consciously choose the appropriate response. Since we're constantly dealing with emotions, Figure T15.2 presents these steps as an iterative cycle.

Emotional Awareness

The first step to maintaining emotional balance—being aware of the emotion—may sound obvious, but it's not always as easy as it sounds. In the midst of our everyday busyness, the mind is already occupied with myriad distractions and mountains of information. In the face of such an onslaught, we may default to suppressing our emotions without even consciously realizing we're doing it. We become aware of our emotions when they're strong enough to move to the forefront of our

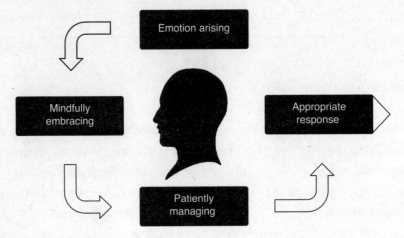

Figure T15.2 The four steps of emotional balance.

awareness. Therefore, acknowledging the emotion exists is the first step to managing it.

Mindful Embrace

The second step in maintaining emotional balance is to mindfully embrace the emotion. In other words, simply notice that the emotion is there and hold it without suppressing or acting on it. Open awareness training, described in Chapter 3, is an invaluable skill for this. Being able to see the emotion as an experience, and not letting it overcome you, diminishes its power. Instead of constantly fighting *against* the emotion, you're able to be *with* it. When it comes to mindful embrace, your breath can be helpful. While observing the emotion, pay attention to your breath; allow its gentle rhythm to calm you.

Patience and Balance

The third step is to apply patience and balance. Patience is about having the courage to face the discomfort of the emotion. Patience will help you endure and contain the emotion, rather than flee from it.

Whereas patience can help you ride out the emotion, balance can keep you neutral. Balance can help you avoid any automatic aversion or attraction you may have toward it. With the ability to embrace the emotion with patience and balance, you can now maintain the focus and clarity necessary to determine the best, most productive response to it.

Appropriate Response

The fourth and final step involves making a decision—choosing the most appropriate response to the situation—based on your awareness of the emotion, your embracing of it, and your patience and balance. Of course, the appropriate response is different in each new situation.

For Thomas, this meant using the steps for maintaining emotional balance in preparation for laying off long-time coworkers. While mindfulness couldn't change the fact that people were about to be laid off, it could change the dynamic of the meetings. It could be the one-second difference between Thomas succumbing to knee-jerk despair or being fully present with the focus and clarity needed to help his staff with relocation opportunities. Because he felt he was genuinely being of service to his team—rather than simply being caught up in his own emotions—Thomas was able to be much more at ease with what could have otherwise been an extremely difficult and emotionally draining experience.

While emotional balance is important for being effective at work, finding a balance between work and life is something many of us struggle with. The last technique focuses on how to use mindfulness to establish greater work life balance.

Tips and Reflections for Emotional Balance

- Although we all express and experience emotions in different ways, there's no denying that we're emotional beings who invariably bring those emotions into the office.
- Take a moment to reflect on how you manage your emotions at work. Do you strive to deny and suppress your emotions? Or do you act them out?
- Consider how facing and embracing your emotions could be of benefit to you, both in terms of your health and your ability to be more effective in your interactions with others.

TECHNIQUE #16

Work-Life Balance

Not too long ago, in an age before e-mails and the Internet, most people could keep work and home fairly separate from each other. When they were at work, they worked, and when they were at home, they did home activities like eating, sleeping, and spending time with family and friends.

But technological advancements mean we can now carry work with us wherever we go. This means the line between "work" and "home" keeps getting blurrier and blurrier, almost to the point of no distinction at all.

This shift from "work-life separation" to "work-life integration" has happened very quickly. In today's work environments, many people take for granted that they can, and perhaps even should, be connected and available 24–7. But work-life integration has significant implications for health, happiness, and state of mind.

This technique outlines the underlying causes of work-life imbalance, as well as provide strategies for mindfully managing them.

Understanding Work-Life Imbalance

Work-life balance is a state of mind. And what constitutes balance for one person is not the same for everyone.

For Lucy, a commercial manager with one of the largest banks in Canada, the sign that her work was taking over, came from the lips of her young daughter. One evening, while reading bedtime stories, Lucy's phone beeped. Almost as a natural reaction, Lucy paused.

Her daughter looked and said, "Go ahead, Mommy. Check your message. I'll just finish reading the story on my own."

In that moment, Lucy realized she was out of balance. She saw she was on autopilot when it came to work. As a result, quite often she wasn't fully present with one of the most important people in her life—not even present enough to read a bedtime story start to finish.

With the help of mindfulness training, it didn't take long for Lucy to recognize the root of the problem. Being "always on" made her feel important, but her blind focus on work was negatively impacting the important relationships in her life.

When people say they're struggling with work-life balance, it means that work is getting in the way of life. It feels like there just isn't enough of a barrier keeping the two from intertwining.

Still, imbalance is only a problem if people perceive it that way or if work negatively impacts other areas of life. For example, just because I choose to stay up late working on a report or proposal doesn't necessarily mean I have a problem with work-life balance. It's only a problem if it negatively impacts my perception of balance or my relationships with other important people like family members and friends. For Lucy, her daughter's innocent comment highlighted the negative crossover.

In working toward better work-life balance, it can be useful to explore the different types of imbalance, as well as the many ways applying mindfulness can be restorative. Let's revisit the Matrix (see Figure T16.1) as a framework for digging deeper into underlying causes of work-life imbalance.

In the first quadrant, many people, like Lucy, may not even be aware they're out of balance. Typically high achievers, these types of people tend to be very effective in what they do. Because they can always be connected to work—and because there's always more they could be doing—folks in quadrant one think it's normal to constantly work. Unaware that their work is negatively impacting other areas of their life, they're often focused on performance to the detriment of

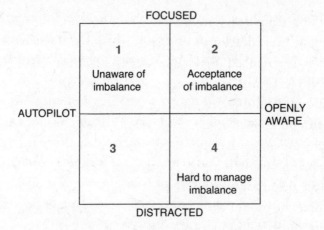

Figure T16.1 Work-Life imbalance and the Matrix.

all else, until family members or persistent health problems shine a spotlight on their unhealthy attachments. In terms of work-life imbalance, people operating in the first quadrant are focused, but on autopilot.

While people in the first quadrant are focused and effective at work, individuals in the third quadrant lack the kind of focus necessary to be effective in either work or life. They spend a lot of time feeling stressed, stretched, and overwhelmed. Unaware of how much work is infiltrating their lives, they're ruled by constant distractions.

In the fourth quadrant, it's no secret that work and life are out of balance. People in quadrant four know they're working too much. They know they're allowing work to get in the way of other important things in life. Yet despite the evidence, they don't feel they have a choice. They're aware of the imbalances, but feel unable to change.

Regardless of where you might place yourself on the Matrix in terms of work-life balance, the question is, "What can be done?" How do you move into the second quadrant, where we learn to manage imbalance?

Managing Imbalance

When it comes to managing work-life balance, there will always be challenges. Issues like a child getting sick the morning of a big presentation or your boss asking you to work on the Saturday you promised to be at your son's soccer game will inevitably arise. There will also be times when work demands prevent you from eating well, sleeping well, or getting enough exercise.

In other words, there will always be moments of imbalance.

In those moments, you have to make difficult choices: Do you stay home with your child, potentially letting the team down for the presentation? Do tell your boss you're unavailable for the Saturday shift? Do you find better ways to take care of yourself, or put it off until a time when work is less demanding—but when it also might be too late?

There are no right or wrong answers to any of these questions. Ultimately, how you manage the imbalances in your life is up to you. But using mindfulness to manage imbalances offers two primary benefits:

- *Focus*—Training in mindfulness helps you feel less overwhelmed by daily tasks and challenges. It helps provide the clarity of mind to accept what you can't change, and make mindful choices about where to place your limited attention—in a way that best serves you and others. Further, it helps you be present with the imbalance, allowing you to sit with the discomfort, observe it, and not let it overwhelm your mind.
- *Awareness*—Training in mindfulness helps you maintain awareness of when you're not in balance. It helps keep you from falling into habitual patterns that are unhealthy, both for yourself and others around you. It also helps you distinguish between what you can and can't control.

In the second quadrant of the Matrix—maintaining both focus and awareness—you develop greater resilience to the realities of life's constant challenges. While those challenges don't just go away, they do become much easier to manage. Mindfulness helps you maintain balance within yourself by accepting life's imbalances. It allows you to let go of things outside of your control, saving all that mental energy to manage things within your control and thereby reducing stress and worry.

Work-Life Balance Strategies

Regular mindfulness training is powerful, so powerful in fact that it rewires your brain, helping you enjoy the good moments in life and build your resilience to imbalance. In addition to regular training, which is covered in Part 3, the following are a few tips to help enhance work-life balance.

Mindful Work-Life Balance

- *Practice Mindfulness Throughout Your Day*—In addition to doing regular, daily mindfulness training, include additional training sessions when you arrive at work, before lunch, before going home, or as was presented in Performance Breaks, even more frequently. This can be a powerful means to monitor your mind, ensure you're clear on your priorities, and sprinkle in small drops of focus, relaxation, and clarity throughout the day.

- *Make Tough Choices*—Better awareness of the imbalances in your work and life allow you to see that you always have choices in the face of challenges. With mindfulness, those choices are made with a calm, clear mind, rather than one that is over-worked, overwhelmed, and on autopilot.

- *Set Boundaries*—Look at the sources of distraction in your life—what creates imbalance between work and family—and set appropriate boundaries. For many, the biggest sources of distraction are the mobile phone and other electronic devices. Set boundaries around when these tools are used and when they're off, both for your own peace of mind and for the quality of your interactions with others. Consider applying boundaries around working in the evenings, on weekends, and during vacation. While you may have to cross a boundary you have set, try to make these the exceptions, not the rule.

- *Plan Time for Yourself*—Spend time identifying what helps you feel refreshed and energized. Evaluate what you do for relaxation and determine whether or not it actually helps you relax. If you feel like you don't have any time for yourself, make time. Everyone needs time for self-care. Inviting other people to join in activities you find rejuvenating can be a great way to take care of yourself and enhance the quality of your relationships.

Think of accepting work-life imbalances in the same way as a kayaker navigates a series of rapids. Sometimes, the rough water pushes your boat to the right, and other times, it pushes you to the left. Sometimes, you may even go under. But with enough practice, you have the skills to quickly right yourself. In the constant act of balance and rebalance, mindfulness can be the difference between being upside down and right side up.

Tips and Reflections for Work-Life Balance

- Work-life balance is a state of mind based on how we perceive and manage the imbalances in our lives.
- Reflect on your current state of work-life balance. Are you aware of any imbalances? Are you looking for ways to accept the imbalances and make changes?
- Consider applying one or two of the work-life balance strategies presented in this technique for a week. Note any impact it has on your work and life.

PART II

Mental Strategies

When you first start mindfulness training, you'll probably notice a lot of interesting things about the nature of your thoughts. Your mind may wander, making it difficult to concentrate on the present. Or your mind may fixate on a thought or experience, seemingly unable to let it go. In general, your mind may default to unhelpful neural patterns, instead of ones beneficial to you and others.

You can change that unhealthy pattern.

There are a number of mental strategies designed to help you manage unhelpful neural reaction patterns, as well as develop new, more effective patterns of behavior. In the moment—in that one second of freedom between thought and action—these strategies can be the difference between helpful or harmful responses (Figure PII.1).

The eight mental strategies covered in this part of the book—presence, patience, kindness, beginner's mind, acceptance, balance, joy, and letting go—are critical to bridging the practice of mindfulness with everyday life, putting you one second ahead of your surroundings, your thoughts, and your emotions.

The more you cultivate these strategies as habits, the faster they'll become part of your default mode of behaving and the calmer and clearer your mind will be.

In Part II, I explore each mental strategy in detail, including how to fit them into your daily life. While it may seem like a lot at first, you

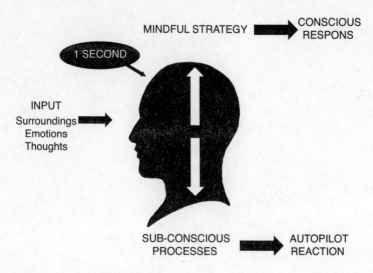

Figure PII.1 Applying mindful strategies.

don't need to master them all overnight. To get the most out of them, try keeping one strategy in mind per week as you implement the techniques from the previous part.

Even better, work one strategy a week into your daily training. For more information on developing and maintaining a daily mindfulness practice, be sure to read Part III. As mentioned earlier, this daily practice is truly the basis of a mindful life.

In a practical sense, the strategies go hand in hand with the Matrix presented in Chapter 1. The more you transform these mental strategies into habits, the more time you'll spend in the second quadrant of the Matrix. And the more time you spend in this quadrant, the more effective and productive you can be at work. Think of these strategies as another layer you can add on top of the techniques to quickly and easily improve your performance at work. They don't replace the techniques—and they certainly don't replace the foundational training methods—but they do mitigate the most persistent thoughts and habits that can prevent you from being your best self moment to moment.

We will start with the powerful strategy of presence.

STRATEGY #1

Presence

Have you ever caught yourself daydreaming during a meeting?

Even worse, have you ever been daydreaming until someone said your name—and then you had no idea why she or he said it, or what the question was?

Or, perhaps less dramatically, have you ever reached the end of a magazine article only to realize that you have no idea what you just read?

These are just a few of the things that can happen when you're not fully present.

Sure, you may often be physically present in a place, but being truly present requires you to fully engage with your current situation: be it a meeting, at a meal, or while reading a book.

Presence is foundational for mindfulness. By definition, being present means we're paying attention to the people, objects, and ideas around us. This level of attention is at the very core of managing focus and awareness—the central characteristics of mindfulness—and maintaining mental effectiveness.

When is the right time to develop or improve your capacity for presence?

No Time Like the Present

Mikel, a country director for a large health-care organization in the Netherlands, was often criticized by his employees for not giving them enough of his time. He always seemed too busy for them, as if any attempt to meet or speak in person were imposing on his valuable time.

For Mikel, the criticism was a source of frustration. He didn't see things the same way. In fact, he felt he was already spending plenty of time with his staff. He even tried to confirm his feelings with hard data. He started tracking every moment he spent with each staff member, and the numbers seemed to corroborate his version of events.

Not surprisingly, the data he presented to his staff didn't do much to change their perceptions.

After taking up daily mindfulness training, though, things changed: Mikel was repeatedly praised by employees for being more available, attentive, and engaged. What really impressed Mikel was that he wasn't actually spending *more* time with his employees. In fact, in terms of quantity, he was spending less time. Even so, the shorter amount of time he spent with his coworkers was qualitatively much better. He was simply more mindful about how he used those moments. He was more present with each person, each question, and each challenge.

Presence has different meanings in terms of social relationships. The word "present" itself can mean "here," "this moment," or "gift." When we're present for others, we embody all three definitions: we're here and in this moment as a gift for other people.

Two minutes with someone who's fully present is more powerful and effective than ten minutes with a distracted person. Just think of how much more productive and effective you could be by being fully present. Like Mikel, you could literally do more, in less time, and get better results.

Make the Most of Now

The past already happened. The future hasn't yet started. Nevertheless, our minds tend to wander between the two. At times, we all have trouble being present in the here and now.

Most people are familiar with the term Attention Deficit Hyperactivity Disorder (ADHD)—a psychiatric condition in which individuals have significant problems maintaining focus. Fewer, though, are familiar with Attention Deficit Trait (ADT)—an unrecognized, though quite real, phenomenon in which brain overload causes individuals to become easily distracted and impatient.[1]

According to researchers, ADHD has a genetic component that can be exacerbated by hectic surroundings. ADT, however, is determined only by surroundings. Nobody is born predisposed to ADT; rather, it's a direct result of our interactions with today's high-pressure, technology-driven reality. As psychiatrist Edward Hallowell wrote, "Just like traffic jams, ADT is a product of modern life. It is created by demands on our time and awareness that have exploded over the past two decades. When our minds are filled with noise, our brains lose the ability to be completely present."[2]

Because of the many distractions in our lives—both internal and external—ADT is endemic to many workplaces, causing even the highest performers to struggle with time management, organization, and prioritizing tasks.[3] Hallowell aptly concluded one study with the comment, "[m]odern office life and an increasingly common condition called 'Attention Deficit Trait' are turning steady executives into frenzied underachievers."[4]

While Hallowell's research was conducted in America, we observe the same tendencies in organizations around the globe. Modern-day workers, regardless of industry and culture, are finding it increasingly difficult to maintain focus in the present moment. From a neurological perspective, people are experiencing a constant neural merry-go-round in the brain (see Figure S1.1).

When we're present, there's strong activity in our prefrontal cortex. As the mind starts to wander, that activity moves towards the back and right side of the brain, to the lateral temporal cortex, the posterior cingulate cortex, and other regions.

As we become aware of our minds wandering, the anterior insula and anterior cingulate cortex deep inside the brain activate. The moment we start to return our attention to the present, the inferior

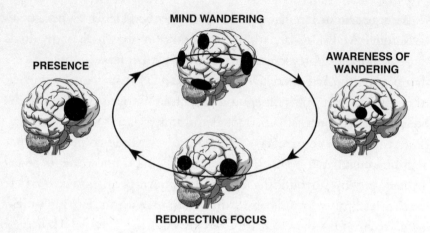

Figure S1.1 The constant neural carousel.

parietal lobe triggers and activity moves back to where it started, in the prefrontal cortex. In this sense, activity goes full circle—from presence, to wandering, and back to presence again.

And it happens again and again, day in and day out, driven by internal and external distractions.

But you don't have to give in to external or internal distractions. You can do something about it. Instead of hopping on the neural carousel, be fully present when you're with other people. Be fully present with your tasks. Be fully present with challenges when they occur.

For some, this kind of mental strategy may seem obvious or overly simplistic. To those people, I say, "Never underestimate the power of presence."

In the Southeast Asia headquarters for a global technology company, for example, marketing and sales employees decided to see what difference it would make if they were intentionally more present in meetings with potential clients. Instead of being concerned with whether they were going to get the sale, what they had to do next, or the number of e-mails piling up in their inbox, these marketing and sales professionals very intentionally focused on the client in front of them. To their delight, they found meetings to be much more successful, not to mention more enjoyable, when they were intentionally present. They also realized just how often their minds wandered and how limiting it can be for effective business relations.

Being present in the moment is the best way to get the most out of your precious time. If you are not present, you are not here and you're trying to multitask. And multitasking, as I established at the beginning of the book, is a myth. You just can't do multiple cognitive tasks at the same time.

None of us can.

Being present helps you be more intentional about what you do and how you live your life. It helps you be the best, most effective version of yourself.

Being present in the moment doesn't require a change in *what you do*. It requires a change in *how you pay attention* to what you do. It's a conscious decision to be present in the moment.

In reality, there is only now.

There is no other time: no past or future. The only time we get anything done is in this moment—this one second. Cultivating presence can help you ensure you make the most out of every now moment.

Mindfulness training is the best way to increase your ability to be more present. By being aware of each breath when you inhale and each breath when you exhale, you are rewiring your brain to pay attention moment to moment.

Be present with your breath, inhaling without thinking about the previous breath or the next breath or the last distraction. Mindfulness training is not ten minutes of awareness. Mindfulness training is awareness of every breath for ten minutes.

Some of us have a desire to reach a particular state of mind during our training or during any activity in life. Yet when we come to a moment with preconceived notions of how we want to be, we've already missed the target. By already being in the future, there is no path to being present. Being present is the path. If you focus on the target, you've missed the moment. If you focus on the path, you've reached the target.

Next, we'll explore the mental strategy of patience, which can be very useful when you are working to rewire your brain and change habits.

Tips and Reflections for Cultivating Presence

- Consider how, when, and why being more present would be of benefit to you.
- Make a conscious decision to intentionally be more present with a colleague, with a client, at a meeting, or at home.
- Note both the benefits and the difficulties in being in that moment. Consider ways to overcome those difficulties to make it easier to be present.

STRATEGY #2

Patience

Lene worked in a European government services organization. Every day, she faced challenges all too common for many of us—how to get herself and her two small children fed, dressed, and out the door without losing her patience.

Lene was conscientious. She got everyone up and moving early in the morning with lots of time for the morning activities. Nevertheless, the same frustrating pattern repeated itself day after day. Just as they were about to leave the house, one of her kids always needed to get something. Or wanted to change clothes. Or was desperate for a snack. Or had to use the bathroom again. Or was upset about something a sibling did.

It wasn't always the same thing, but it was always *something*.

Even though Lene knew the pattern well, she would still react with frustration. Instead of giving her children space and attention as the situation demanded, she became stressed and annoyed. She would often raise her voice, even though it only made the situation worse. It made her upset and drained her energy. By the time she got to work, she was already feeling tired and overwhelmed.

For Lene, practicing patience as a mental strategy made a world of difference. With more insight into the underlying causes of her reaction patters and some ideas for alternative options, Lene was inspired to change her behavior.

Of course, this story is not unique to Lene. Life is full of challenges; it constantly tests our patience. Sometimes, we subconsciously react to difficulties based on patterns deeply embedded in our brain. The end result is not always positive. Patience, or the ability to endure discomfort, can be an effective strategy for choosing a rational response rather than an impulsive reaction. As an old saying goes, "A moment of patience in a moment of anger saves you a thousand moments of regret." While this applies to life in general, work is certainly no exception.

To better understand the neurology behind our patterns of reaction, it's useful to take a look at our triune brain.

The Triune Brain

The human brain is made up of three parts—and thus the term triune, which means three in one. Those three parts are the reptilian brain, the limbic brain, and the cortex (see Figure S2.1).[1]

About 225 million years old, the reptilian brain formed during our early evolution and is the oldest part of the organ. The reptilian brain is focused on our basic needs for survival.

The next-oldest part of the brain, the limbic system, is about 170 million years old. When we began to be "caring beings"—individuals concerned with the well-being of our offspring—the limbic system was the cause. It's also the source of our feelings and moods.

A mere 40 million years old, the cortex was the last area of the brain to develop. It's where we do our rational, intellectual, and logical thinking. It's the home of our conscious awareness.

When we feel threatened, the amygdala—part of our limbic system—triggers our "fight or flight" response. It's often call an amygdala hijack—the hijacking of the rational functioning of the rest

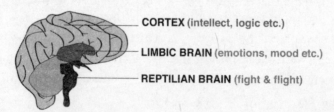

Figure S2.1   The triune brain.

of our brain, making our actions hard to control. In fight or flight mode, our bodies prepare either to physically defend ourselves against an imminent threat or run away.

The fight or flight reflex helped keep us alive during our early evolution and can still do the same when we find ourselves in a dangerous situation. Although most of us rarely find ourselves in imminent physical danger today, life is still full of situations in which we feel threatened. Precisely because these situations seldom pose a physical danger, making a rational, conscious choice is better for our relationships, productivity, health, and well-being than making an automatic, subconscious decision.

Life is full of situations that "threaten" your schedule, your plans, your goals, or your intentions. Still, you don't have to let the ancient, reptilian part of your brain take control. You have evolved; you have a cortex. The cortex allows you to come up with logical and rational solutions—the cortex offers patience.

Fight, Flight, or Patience

Patience involves choosing to stay calm in the face of challenging situations, even when our fight or flight reflex might already be triggered. It's the ability to endure unpleasantness, to confront the situation directly and handle it sensibly, rather than on impulse. Patience is more concerned with larger goals than temporary, quick-fix solutions.

While fight or flight attempts to solve problems by changing external circumstances—by fighting them or running away from them—patience gives us the clarity needed to solve modern problems at the source: namely, in the mind. By disassembling internal reaction patterns, patience gets us one second ahead so that we can see clearly and act appropriately. Patience is the direct path to living a more effective life that's focused on the roots of problems instead of the symptoms.

Of course, patience doesn't come naturally to everyone. Some of us feel the urge to fight or flee more strongly than others. But, be assured, the courage to endure unpleasant situations is a skill that can be developed and nurtured. With mindfulness training, we start to perceive and process reality more through our cortex—the rational, intellectual, and logical part of our brains—and much less through our reptilian brain. We can then rewire our brain to make being patient more and more our default mode of operating—it gets easier and easier.

Once you begin your daily mindfulness training as outlined in Part III, there will be moments when you feel restless. Your inner voice may be saying, "Why am I sitting here not doing anything? I have so many things I need to do." This is a perfect opportunity to train patience. Instead of giving in, find the courage to tolerate the restlessness.

Face restlessness head-on. Don't follow the impulse to get up or suppress the feeling. If you flee from it, you can be sure that it will come up again at another point. An unpleasant experience can only be truly solved where it occurs—in the mind.

Next we'll explore the strategy of kindness which can be a lot more strategic than you might think.

Tips and Reflections for Cultivating Patience

- Consider whether being more patient would be of benefit to you and why. Would it be beneficial at work or at home?
- Reflect on specific situations that trigger your fight-flight response and cause you to be impatient.
- The next time you face one of those situations, stop and take a breath. Keep focusing on your breath until you can feel yourself calming down. See if you can notice whether your reptilian brain or your cortex is currently driving your behavior.
- If it's something that happens regularly, try to welcome it as a great opportunity to practice being patient.
- Be sure to be patient with yourself as you do this. It takes effort to rise above anger or frustration: consciously try to do so.

Kindness

We all want to be happy—and no one wants to suffer. But we don't always act in our best interests or in the best interests of others. How and why people do things that create even their own suffering vary from person to person.

Take a moment to consider what this means for you.

If it's true we all want to be happy and no one wants to suffer, what do we need from other people to be happy? Often the answer is simple: things like presence, attention, respect, understanding, and acceptance. What do other people need from us to be happy?

The exact same things.

In this way, we're all experts in making each other happy.

What Does It Mean to Be Kind?

Odds are, you've heard of the golden rule: do unto others as you would have them do unto you. A fundamental pillar of mindfulness isn't too far off from that age-old adage: "May I be happy—and may I do what I can so you can be happy." This pillar can also be summed up by the word kindness.

In truth, we're all already experts in what makes others happy. But if we all want to be happy and we're all experts in knowing how to make each other happy, why aren't we always happy together? The most common reason is that we live busy lives and often forget to do things we fundamentally know are important, namely, respecting ourselves and others, and looking out for our own happiness and the happiness of others. In the midst of our deadlines and demands, we forget kindness.

Now, kindness isn't always about pleasing others and being nice. One of the kindest things you can do for another person is give honest, constructive feedback. You aren't doing anybody any favors by letting them think they're performing at a higher level than they are in reality. In my own experience, even firing people can be an act of kindness. And if done with kindness as the driving motivation, the experience for everyone involved will be dramatically improved.

In addition, kindness can be beneficial for the bottom line. For example, consider the business drivers for a global management consulting firm. When organizations hire consultants, on the surface, it's in order to tap into their knowledge and skills. For knowledge and skills to translate into results, though, it requires effective human interactions.

During a program with a group of consultants in New York, the question was put on the table, "How would more kindness be of benefit to your daily work?" The group paused for a moment as kindness is not necessarily something that people talk a lot about in high-pressure, high-performing, fast-thinking consulting firms in New York!

After a while, one of the participants suggested that perhaps having an explicit intention to be kind to their clients could enhance the effectiveness of their work and the ability of their clients to implement their recommendations. In this light, the consulting group saw kindness as a potential competitive edge. They decided to test setting an explicit intention of being kind to their clients and see how that would change their approach and the outcomes. Through this exercise, they found setting an intention to be kind made client meetings easier, more productive and more enjoyable. They also found kindness to have a significant and positive impact on themselves as professionals, colleagues, friends, and family members.

In fact, it is not just other people who benefit from our kindness. Kindness can be one of the most effective ways of looking after yourself. As the direct neurological opposite to unpleasant states of mind, kindness doesn't just pacify negative tendencies; rather, it pulls them up by the roots.

There is no room for anger in a mind that is being kind.

The Science of Kindness

Kindness has a scientifically documented positive effect on both your mental and physical well-being.[1] When you're kind, your immune system is stronger, you become more creative, you have better social relationships, and you increase your enjoyment of life. While anger—the opposite of kindness—also has long-lasting effects, they're generally not very positive outcomes: a greater risk of heart attack, chronic headaches, an increase in a variety of other illnesses, and a statistically shorter life.[2]

Martin Seligman, a leading positive psychology researcher, noted in one study that the impact of performing friendly acts toward other people can be measured in your own level of happiness for up to eight weeks after the event.[3] Before we're kind to others, though, we need to be kind to ourselves. If we are not kind to ourselves, it's difficult, if not impossible, to be genuinely kind to others.

Think about the airline safety instructions you always hear before takeoff: "In case of an emergency, put on your own oxygen mask before assisting others." Why should you help yourself first? Because you can't be of much service to others if you pass out. There's nothing heroic about losing consciousness trying to help others.

In much the same way, the first step in developing kindness is to show kindness to yourself. Give yourself a break. Don't beat yourself up over missteps or mistakes. Instead, treat yourself how you'd like to be treated, with understanding and respect. When you're kind and caring to yourself, it then becomes possible to be truly kind to others.

We have tremendous power to choose not only how we live our lives but also how our brain is wired to respond to stimuli in our environment. If we allow ourselves to constantly respond to frustrations with anger, our minds default to a pattern of responding with anger. If we train ourselves to respond with kindness, however, our default neurological reaction becomes kindness. We all have the freedom to cultivate the qualities we want to amplify and strengthen in our lives. We all have anger and kindness; it's up to us to decide which one to nurture.

To increase your capacity for kindness toward yourself and others, incorporate the cultivation of kindness into your daily mindfulness efforts. This includes both in the office with your colleagues and while you pursue more formal mindfulness training.

The next strategy explores the beauty of a beginner's mind.

Tips and Reflections for Cultivating Kindness

- Consider what benefit more kindness could have for you at work or at home. Think about what it might look like and why it would be beneficial.
- Practice applying kindness in these situations and see what happens.
- Consider expanding kindness to be the lens through which you experience everything—in the office, at home, throughout your community. Let it be a fundamental attitude for yourself and everything you experience as much as possible.
- When you're doing your mindfulness training, let yourself and whatever you experience be wrapped in an attitude of kindness.
- The more you think this way and train this way, the stronger kindness as a mental modus operandi becomes due to the creation of stronger neural connections related to it.

STRATEGY #4

Beginner's Mind

Years ago, I took a walk in the woods with my children. As we were walking, one of my boys shouted out in excitement. I went over to find him holding a piece of birch bark in his hand. I have to admit, it didn't look particularly special to me.

For him, though, the bark was a treasure. He explained it was a perfect canvas and he wanted to paint on it when we got home.

When my other son came to see the big discovery, he got excited, too, taking the piece of bark and throwing it into the air. The bark flew through the air like a glider. He gleefully shouted, "The perfect airplane!"

When the bark landed, my daughter picked it up. Delighted, she cried, "Boat!" She knelt down by a little stream and pushed her vessel into the water.

What for me was just a piece of ordinary bark was at the same time a canvas for painting, a plane, and a boat.

Where I was a victim of my own limited and habitual perceptions, my children saw potential and possibilities. The Japanese have a word for this ability: *mitate*. Translated, it means "looking at something anew."

In my experience, looking anew is foundational for business success. Without the ability to do so, we default to yesterday's perception of the market and the competition. We become complacent—and might just wake up to find ourselves behind the bus. Just ask Nokia about their famous decline, from 49.4 percent global market share in 2007, to a humiliating 3 percent in 2013.

How did it happen? One 2007 statement, from their current CEO, Olli-Pekka Kallasvuo, sums it up: "From a competitor point of view, the iPhone is nothing but a niche product." It turns out history—and the market—would beg to differ.

In mindfulness training, we call the ability to see things with a fresh perspective "the beginner's mind." And it was a lack of beginner's mind that caused Nokia to neglect a new product and nearly end up bankrupt.

A few natural traits stand between each of us and a beginner's mind: namely, *habitual perception* and *cognitive rigidity*.

We've Seen It All Before

Imagine you're looking at a rose for the first time.

You notice its color, how soft its petals feel, its sweet fragrance, and its thorns, as if you'd never seen anything like it.

The first time, your mind creates a mental picture of this new object, filing it under "rose."

The next time you see a rose, it takes hardly any time for the mind to recognize it. As your mind associates the rose with your mental picture of a rose, you become more likely to see the image in your memory as opposed to the actual object in front of you.

Rather than seeing this individual rose as what it is, your mind quickly categorizes it as "another rose."

Other animals experience something similar. For example, one group of researchers placed individual rats at the door of a small labyrinth. With a click, the labyrinth opened, allowing the rat to enter and search for a piece of chocolate.

During the first few rounds of the experiment, the rats' brain activity stayed high as they explored the labyrinth. But, after just a few rounds, brain activity diminished, spiking only at the initial click and the chocolate discovery (see Figure S4.1). The rats had developed habitual perception; they no longer perceived the labyrinth in the same way.[1]

This is not necessarily a bad thing. Life would be pretty overwhelming if we didn't have the ability to quickly recognize things

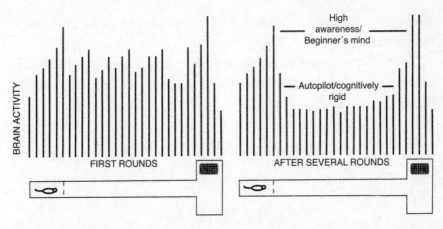

Figure S4.1 Development of habitual perception.

we've seen before. In evolution, this is called pattern recognition, and it represents one of the greatest strengths of the human mind. Just think: you wouldn't get much done if, every time you needed to write something, you had to figure out what a pen was and how it worked.

Still, the automatic association between what's actually in front of you and what you've seen in the past—the neurological process called habitual perception—can be problematic. It means you often don't actually *see* what's right there in front of you.

In fact, what you do see has much less to do with actual reality, and much more to do with the reality your mind creates based on your history and habits. In other words, you have programmed yourself to see reality in a certain way. Every rose is the same rose.

And roses aren't the only things we habitually perceive.

In our interactions with other people, our work, and ourselves, we often limit ourselves to restricted perceptions—to what we know and have known. We become cognitively rigid. It happened to me when I was walking in the woods with my children, and it happened to the CEO of Nokia when he first held an iPhone.

Cognitive rigidity—the inflexibility created by automatically recalling our habitual perceptions—is not conducive to creativity. It doesn't help us innovate. Or help us to see new solutions to old challenges, let alone new solutions to *new* challenges. On the contrary, cognitive rigidity hinders our effectiveness and performance, both personally and professionally.

Thankfully, none of us are doomed to cognitive rigidity, or habitual perception. Seeing things anew—with a beginner's mind—can be a proactive choice.

Unlearning Habitual Perceptions

At work and at home, how often do the same challenges come up time and time again?

What if, instead of seeing these challenges the same way every time, we viewed them with fresh eyes? Would we confront those challenges more effectively?

Science seems to think so.

In one study, researchers from Ben-Gurion University looked at the impact of mindfulness training on cognitive rigidity. Specifically, they evaluated how a group of people solved a series of problems.

Researchers initially presented participants with problems that required a complex formula to solve. Later, they presented a series of problems that were much easier. After solving the hard problem with a complex formula, participants then had trouble seeing any easier way.

Albert Einstein is known to have said, "A problem cannot be solved with the same level of mind that created it." He may have been onto something.

In a sense, participants in the study were "blinded" by their experience of needing a complex formula. Even though the later problems were much easier, earlier experience blocked them from seeing any simpler solutions.

After undergoing eight weeks of mindfulness training, though, the scores of those same people significantly improved. Their minds were less rigid, making them better able to see the actual reality of problems before them, rather than their habitual perception.[2]

But what is it about mindfulness training that makes the mind less rigid?

It's that one second of space, that one second of freedom, that Jacob identified in Chapter 1. That one second is the difference between defaulting to habitual patterns and taking a moment to choose to see a situation as it actually is.

Mindfulness training shows us that we don't have to give in to our habitual perceptions. Our automatic associations don't have to be so automatic. In that one second between seeing a rose in front of us and associating it with our mental image, we can choose to see the rose anew.

The ability to face reality as it is—or at least not be stuck in old ways of seeing things—is the essence of a beginner's mind. Without a beginner's mind, we lock ourselves inside our own experience; we stagnate in our mind's habitual perception. With a beginner's mind, we see things with fresh eyes and an open mind.

Thankfully, the choice is ours.

Choosing a Beginner's Mind

Extremely powerful applications of Beginner's Mind arose during a program with an Environmental Health and Safety Team on-site in the Alberta Oil Sands as part of a mindfulness training program at a large Canadian energy company. One of the team's primary functions is to ensure people work in accordance with environmental health and safety standards. Knowing how easy it is for people to see things with habitual minds was very impactful for the team.

They realized that many of the ways they presented safety messages were not necessarily conducive to people paying attention and maintaining alertness for potential hazards or threats. They looked at how they could be more open minded in how they presented messages and conducted investigations. They also discussed ways they could enhance overall safety by helping on-site personnel increase awareness and overcome cognitive rigidity.

Realizing their habitual tendencies and *choosing* the perspective of a beginner's mind had a significantimpact on their work. Rather than default to the tried and supposedly true, the team began looking at old problems as if they were new. They no longer presumed they already held the answers; rather, they were intentionally open minded, freeing themselves to see situations as they were rather than through the lens of habitual perception.

Cultivating a beginner's mind can be a wonderful way to change how you experience life. Regardless of your work environment, daily life can be filled with more wonders and possibilities when you see things with a fresh perspective.

The next strategy explores the benefits of acceptance.

Tips and Reflections for Cultivating a Beginner's Mind

- Think about people or tasks in your life that you tend to see negatively. Consider whether having a beginner's mind could be beneficial for you and for them.
- Try applying a beginner's mind to these situations. Note any change in how you experience them. Notice any improvement in your interaction or effectiveness.
- Challenge yourself to be more curious in your day-to-day activities. Be open to what is happening to you moment to moment. The less you presume to know, the more your mind will open.

STRATEGY #5

Acceptance

For a year, the marketing team at a large Danish retail chain worked on a new campaign. They spent hours and hours, tweaking and plotting until all was just right. Not long before they were supposed to launch the campaign, they discovered another division within the company was planning a launch for the same time.

Uh-oh.

It was immediately clear that both campaigns couldn't move forward. It just didn't make sense for two areas of the company to compete with each other. As you might imagine, this caused no small amount of anger and frustration on the part of the team who now felt like they had wasted an entire year.

I asked the group if they'd done everything they could to change the situation.

Of course they had, they said.

I then asked them if steps had been taken to prevent something similar from happening again in the future.

Again, the answer was, "Of course."

Finally, I asked if there was anything more they could do to fix the problem.

Dejected, they said they'd exhausted all options. It was over.

As chance would have it, the topic of discussion for that week was acceptance. After looking at their situation with an accepting mind

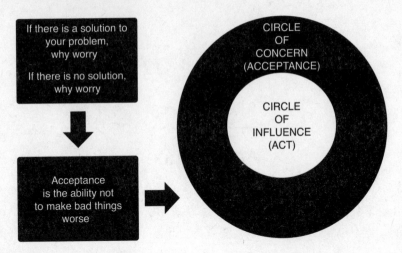

Figure S5.1   Circle of influence.

state they were able to let go of their frustration and cultivate a greater sense of calm.

Acceptance is the ability to refrain from making an already difficult situation more difficult. As the team realized, if you *can* solve the problem, why worry? Likewise, if you *can't* solve the problem, why worry?

A good framework for looking at this is to consider what is in your circle of influence versus what is in your circle of concern—see Figure S5.1.

If there is a problem that you can do something about, then you should act as if it is within your circle of influence. If there is a problem that you really cannot do anything about, don't make it worse by fighting it.

A situation is as it is.

Accept it and move on, without carrying on an inner battle.

Zero Resistance

There is a neurological tendency to resist things we don't like, even if there's nothing we can do to change them. In a way, we're programmed to hold on to frustrating things. Even though we know it would be far healthier to let them go, we have difficulty accepting things that annoy us.

$$P \times R = S$$

Figure S5.2   The arithmetic of suffering.

Suffering doesn't exist on its own, independent of us. In fact, we contribute quite a lot to it. Consider the formula presented in Figure S5.2, where P stands for pain, R for resistance, and S for suffering:

Imagine yourself in a situation that has ten units of pain (the number doesn't much matter, nor does how you quantify it). In addition, you resist the pain in equal measure, with ten units of resistance. Ultimately, your suffering will be at 100. However you look at it, 100 units of suffering is significantly higher than no suffering at all.

Now, what happens if in the same situation, you simply offer zero resistance? Even if you began with 1,000 units of pain, zero resistance makes your suffering zero.

Pain in life is inevitable. That's a stark reality of existence.

The degree to which you suffer from it, however, is optional. When you gain acceptance, you increase both mental space and focus for things you can actually do something about. You stop worrying about the things you can't change and, instead, you concentrate on the things you can change.

Acceptance Is Power

Acceptance is a powerful way to increase your effectiveness—not to mention your happiness—just by changing the way you perceive obstacles and challenges.

To be clear, acceptance doesn't equate to being a doormat, giving up, or being apathetic. It's not passivity. By all means, if you can do something to improve or change your situation, do it. If you can't change the situation, however, then why waste mental resources trying to think up a way to alter the unavoidable or inevitable?

But how do you know? How can you tell the difference between a situation where you should keep fighting to make a change versus letting go and accepting the situation as it is?

In many work scenarios, this "tipping point" can be difficult to determine. The key is to remember that acceptance as a mental strategy is not necessarily about what you do or what you don't do; rather, it is about how you experience and perceive the world around you. I can accept that I may not be able to achieve world peace in my lifetime, but it doesn't mean I won't continue to try. It means I will do so with a calm, clear, accepting mind.

We have the freedom to influence many things in our lives. But some things simply can't be changed. With acceptance, we cease to make difficult situations worse by dwelling on the unchangeable. This is a great platform for the next mental strategy of Balance.

Tips and Reflections for Cultivating Acceptance

- Consider how being more accepting of things you can't change would be beneficial to you. Think of specific situations in which you find acceptance difficult.
- The next time you confront a frustrating or disheartening situation at work, ask yourself, Did I do everything I could to fix this problem? If the answer is "yes," then consciously accept it and move on. The more you do this, the easier it will become.
- Consider what the difference in acceptance versus apathy means for you. Are there things that you accept too easily? Are there things you don't accept enough?
- Mindfulness training is a great way to cultivate acceptance. As you sit in stillness, relate to anything you are experiencing with an accepting attitude. If you're restless, your resistance will make the situation more difficult. Relate to the restlessness with acceptance.

STRATEGY #6

Balance

Freedom is a state of mind. Not a place. Not a situation. Freedom releases a flow of mental space and effectiveness. Sue realized that clearly when she was halfway through a mindfulness program in a large community services not-for-profit company in Australia. As the Head of Human Resources with two small children at home, Sue had a busy life with many demands on her time and attention. Cultivating the mental strategy of balance gave her the insight to create freedom in the middle of her busy life. To help understand what we mean by balance, let's look at how it changed Sue's experience of her life without her changing his surroundings.

Sue's mind was being bombarded with approximately 11 million bits of information per second.[1] You experience the same every single second. Most of this information comes through your eyes and the remainder through your other senses. Out of the many bits of information, there are around seven that you are able to consciously pay attention to in any given moment. The rest remain outside of your conscious awareness—although they are still very much present in your subconscious awareness and therefore have the ability to influence your thinking and behavior. Going back to the seven bits that you can attend to, there are three possible reactions: you like it; you don't like it; or you are neutral toward it.

In Sue's case there were specific things that entered into her conscious awareness that she liked. She liked getting good feedback from the CEO and her colleagues, feeling respected, getting a convenient car park at work, and obedient behavior from her children. There were also things she didn't like. She did not like criticism, negative feedback from clients about her staff, cold weather, or last-minute changes in schedules for her kids.

You can no doubt recognize similar patterns in yourself. All your experiences are judged in these categories. But it doesn't stop there. Every single little judgment leads to a neurological reaction. The natural reaction to something you like is wanting more, and the reaction to something you don't like is to try to push it away. Like Sue wanting more positive feedback and resisting criticisms.

Take a moment to consider how this might apply to you. Think of the last time you ate a nice piece of chocolate or something else you really like. Were you satisfied after the first bite and put the rest down, or did you want more to the extent that your thoughts were already consumed by taking the next bite? Try to imagine you are offered a nice piece of chocolate, and just before you put your teeth into it, it is taken out of your hands and thrown away. How do you feel? Do you have a feeling of satisfaction and a feeling that everything is fine? Or are you experiencing resistance? This is a natural reaction pattern, and it can be explained by looking at one of the brain's neurochemical processes, particularly our production of, and desire for, dopamine.

Hooked on Dopamine

Neurotransmitters are chemicals that transmit signals between brain cells. Two of the most important neurotransmitters are dopamine and serotonin (see Figure S6.1). Together, they account for the "attraction/rejection" reactions we experience in day-to-day life.

Dopamine is a reward substance that causes us to feel joy, satisfaction, and fulfillment. Every time we get something we like, the brain releases dopamine. It makes us feel good. It's the reason why, after having something we like, we want more. While dopamine can be nice for obvious reasons, it also has a dark side: dopamine is addictive. All forms of addiction—whether to gambling, drugs, overeating, or praise from your boss—are based on the desire for a dopamine rush.

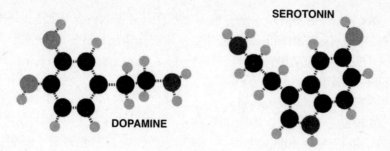

SEROTONIN

DOPAMINE

Figure S6.1   The chemical makeup of dopamine and serotonin.

If praise is your drug of choice, each pat on the back you receive is accompanied by a release of dopamine. You may find, then, your enjoyment or frustration at work to be heavily influenced by other people. And much of your energy and effectiveness are likely dependent on attaining things you like, as well as avoiding things you dislike.

Fortunately, our happiness need not depend on our surroundings. We can actually avoid falling victim to our own dopamine addictions. Another neurotransmitter, serotonin, has a wide-ranging impact on the mind and body, primarily serving to inhibit impulsive behavior and increase relaxation and clarity.

Boosting Serotonin

Serotonin and dopamine are closely connected. When they're in balance, we can enjoy good food, or a glass of wine, or praise without becoming addicted. Serotonin balances out the negative effect of dopamine, enabling us to be more resilient in the face of adversity, be that criticism or even physical or emotional pain.

So how can we create more serotonin—and experience more peace and freedom as a result? Research shows mindfulness training to be one way to increase the levels of serotonin in your brain.[2]

When you stop yourself from following an impulse—say, quitting after one serving of your favorite food or drink—serotonin balances out the dopamine release. In your daily mindfulness training, you're constantly resisting impulses to follow distracting thoughts or hold onto stress. You're training your ability to observe your own experiences, giving you the mental space to deliberately choose responses rather than react on autopilot. Every time you successfully inhibit automatic reactions, your serotonin level increases.

Does this mean you become someone who doesn't enjoy anything in life?

Quite the opposite. It means you can enjoy the things you truly enjoy without developing an all-encompassing desire or addiction. It means you can respond more skillfully to things you don't like without becoming angry and aggressive. You attain greater balance.

Chances are, once you start regular mindfulness training, you will notice an increase in calm and a decrease in impulsive reactions. The more you train yourself to resist automatic impulses, the more in balance your dopamine and serotonin levels become. And balance is genuine freedom—freedom that comes from within. Balance is also a great foundation for the next mental strategy of Joy.

Tips and Reflections for Cultivating Balance

- When you feel an impulse to pursue something you like, pause for a moment to let your serotonin balance out any release of dopamine.
- Consciously identify the tasks at work that bring your instant gratification—say answering an e-mail or text. Now identify the tasks that bring discomfort. This may be fielding complaints from customers or confronting a surly coworker. Be aware of your reactions to these tasks and temper those reactions by purposefully limiting or delaying the gratification of the experiences you like, while more actively confronting the experiences you dislike.
- Once you begin mindfulness training, be aware of your reactions to what you experience. The simple exercise of observing your breath can be a source of joy and peace, resulting in a desire to stay that way. In this moment, you are at risk of being bound by an attachment to something you like. At other times,

you will be distracted by a specific thought or experience that creates discomfort or pain. In that moment, you are at risk of being bound by a resistance to something you don't like.

- You train balance by being aware of your reaction to everything you experience, good, bad, and neutral. Notice the experiences you like and those you do not like, things where you experience attraction and things where you experience aversion.

- Just being aware of these reactions will lead to change. When you become aware of a desire, the desire will lessen as it's replaced by awareness of the desire. When you become aware of resistance, the resistance will lessen as it's replaced by awareness of it. If something is pleasant and nice, you observe it neutrally without giving it more value or holding onto it. If something is unpleasant, you observe it neutrally without wanting it to disappear.

Joy

Before we dive into joy, let's start with a little exercise. Take a moment to think of someone you really like.

Now close your eyes and picture their face. Reflect on how much you like them and how they make you feel. Now notice what you are experiencing in this moment in your body and in your mind. How did you feel?

Was it pleasant or unpleasant? Easy or difficult? Was your mind open or closed? Light or dark? Would you like more of it or not?

Now take a moment to think of someone you really do not like.

Again, close your eyes and picture them standing right in front of you. Think about how much you don't like them and how they make you feel. Experience it for a moment. Again, notice what you are experiencing in this moment in your body and your mind.

How did you feel?

Was it pleasant or unpleasant? Easy or difficult? Was your mind open or closed? Light or dark? Would you like more of it or not?

We can learn three things from this simple exercise:

- Negative states of mind, such as anger or frustration, do not make us feel good physically.
- Positive states of mind, such as happiness and joy, do feel good.
- Feelings such as anger and joy are not necessarily dependent on what our surroundings throw at us. We can evoke them at will.

Feelings come from within. As you just proved to yourself, we can choose anger or happiness or any other feeling simply by thinking about things that make us feel that emotion. This means, by extension, we can choose to be happy or we can choose to be angry. We can awaken feelings and cultivate them in almost any situation.

Joy is no exception. And there are lots of good reasons for cultivating more joy in life.

Joy boosts our energy and performance; it enhances our ability to do good work and excel at business. Like all feelings, joy is something we can enable inside ourselves.

Before we turn to cultivating joy as a powerful mental strategy, let's take a look at the impact of joy as opposed to anger on our nervous system.

Mind-Body Connections

Our nervous system reacts to our state of mind. What we feel mentally has a significant effect on our physical body.

In particular, when we're feeling threatened or stressed, our sympathetic nervous system goes into "fight or flight" mode—the same physical mode we'd be in if we were in serious danger. When we're relaxed and at ease, our parasympathetic nervous system puts the body into "rest and digest" mode. This is not unlike the feeling you might have after a good meal. In this state, we're more open to enjoying the moment.

Understanding the impact of our mental state on our body is important for enhancing both well-being and performance. Cultivating joy enables us to rebalance our nervous system when we're faced with a perceived threat, giving us that extra one second between responding rashly and responding with clarity and calm. It can also help us sleep better and digest food more effectively.

Quite simply, joy equates to taking better care of both body and mind. When we're happy doing something, we expand both our mental and physical resources. We become better at solving problems, we're more at ease, and we learn faster. Our social skills are strengthened, making it easier to build new social connections and strengthen existing ones.

Our physical strengths are increased and our health improves. From a psychological point of view we develop more stability and optimism.[1]

For some, the notion of joy can sound unrealistic or overly optimistic. Resist the urge to think this way. Joy can have a powerful impact on your nervous system and is relatively easy to cultivate.

Joy is also contagious.

Mirroring

In a study published in the *British Medical Journal*,[2] researchers found happiness to be a collective phenomenon. In other words, happiness is not something we only enjoy on our own. In fact, researchers found that happiness can be traced to three degrees of separation. When you're happy, it has an infectious—and measurable—effect on the people around you. In other words, not only does joy have a positive impact on your own nervous system but it also helps others feel calm and relaxed.

Humans are highly social beings. Consciously or subconsciously, we look to the people around us for cues to how we should behave and feel in any given situation. Scientists have identified what they call "mirror neurons"[3] in the brain that underlie our tendency to copy or reflect what someone else is feeling. It's the reason a laughing baby might cause us to smile or seeing someone we love in pain may cause us to tear up.

If you're with someone who's joyful, it's neurologically infectious. In contrast, if you're with someone who's upset, depressed, or angry, that can also spread.

Given how easily our behavior can impact others in our environment, it's worth pausing to think about the ways positive emotions like joy can be beneficial to you, your colleagues, and your organization. When you bring anxiety, stress, irritation, and frustration into your work environment, it's important to consider your impact on your colleagues.

To be clear, I'm not suggesting it's always easy to be joyful—nor should we be hard on ourselves when we feel angry or upset. We all lead busy lives with many demands competing for our time and attention. Positive states of mind can easily drown in the ocean of everyday activities that make up much of our daily lives.

But fortunately, we can train ourselves to have more joy in our lives. We don't need to wait for it to find us—we can proactively choose joy.

Fostering Joy

At a medium-sized not-for-profit health-care organization in Singapore, the idea of enabling joy generated a lot of discussion.

Initially, there was pushback as to whether or not joy was really relevant in the work place, especially in an environment working to support people with serious health issues. One leader—the chief financial officer—felt very strongly that joy was something she experienced at home and when she went shopping, and that it had little to do with work. She was also concerned that being joyful in the face of other people's suffering would somehow be wrong.

Other leaders challenged her with the potential benefits of fostering joy within their teams. They realized joy didn't have to mean skipping down the halls. Instead, staff could find joy in being of service to others.

Collectively, the group decided that fostering more joy would be the best way to reduce stress and enhance presence and kindness in patient care. Intentionally, bringing more joy into the work place became a strategic focus for them.

In the exercise at the beginning of this strategy, we experienced that we can foster joy spontaneously within ourselves. We can do the same in the middle of our busy lives. The office is a terrific place to enable joy, as is your daily mindfulness training. Now, we will look at the final strategy of Letting Joy.

Tips and Reflections for Cultivating Joy

- Joy is straightforward. The only thing you have to do is find joy in sitting still. In a smile or laugh. In the moments that make up a day.
- Most of us are "always on," always connected, always running from one thing to the next. The key to cultivating joy is to enjoy

your daily activities. This is especially true if and when you embark on daily mindfulness training—see it as a gift you're giving yourself every day.

- In your mindfulness training, give yourself the opportunity to let go of your task lists and ambitions. Let go of performing. Let yourself sit, value each breath, celebrate each moment—with joy. The few minutes a day you think about these strategies are your time. Enjoy them with a smile.

STRATEGY #8

Letting Go

Marie was responsible for designing a complex new organizational structure for her division of a large European financial services company. This meant the future of several hundred jobs—and people—was in her hands.

Marie was very much aware of the responsibility she had to all those people. She was so aware, in fact, she carried the burden home with her at night. This distraction made it hard for Marie to be present with her family.

When Marie went to bed, she was exhausted. Even though she desperately needed sleep, thoughts about work kept her tossing and turning all night.

Most of us have experienced a similar problem: being unable to shut off our minds long enough to fall asleep. Some of us struggle with leaving thoughts behind when we move from one task to the next. Still others have difficulties transitioning from work to home.

Mindfulness training can strengthen your ability to let go of a thought before it leads to more related thoughts. In fact, the better we become at letting thoughts go, the lighter and more flexible our minds become. In a way, it's similar to how your computer performs better after you've cleaned up the hard drive or emptied the cache. Letting go reduces the clutter in your mind.

One Tibetan word eloquently describes the challenge of letting go: *nam-tok*.

Nam-Tok

Imagine you are lying on a beach a long way from home. Suddenly, a thought about a work responsibility comes into your mind. This is a *nam*, a stand-alone thought that occurs in the mind.

But the mind rarely stops there.

Tok is the Tibetan word for each thought that spontaneously occurs as a result of the first thought. If your work *nam* started with a looming deadline, the related *toks* might have to do with approaching milestones or tasks yet to be completed. There are often several *toks* that arise with each *nam*. In fact, there can be a whole cascade of additional thoughts, depending on how our mind reacts to the initial *nam*.

For Marie, the *toks* were the root of her problem. Rather than the initial thought, all the unnecessary and unhelpful resulting thoughts kept her awake when she needed sleep. And her lack of sleep further reduced her focus at work and her presence with her family. It was a self-perpetuating cycle.

But Marie made a plan to let go.

As part of a larger program within her company, she started training in mindfulness for ten minutes a day. On top of that, she began to observe where these relentless floods of thoughts started, intending to pull them up by the roots. Typically, her thoughts started racing as soon as her alarm clock went off in the morning. To alter the destructive cycle, she decided to let the alarm clock remind her to let go of thoughts. Before getting out of bed, she did five minutes of mindfulness training. Five minutes of mental training gave her the clarity to get out of bed with a more calm, clear, and present mind.

After a few months of practice, Marie found it much easier to let go of intrusive thoughts. She could now get through her morning routine without feeling stressed or overwhelmed. Beginning the day with a calm, clear mind made for a much better start to her day. It also resulted in a better night's sleep and made her more present and available for her kids.

Letting go is a simple but very powerful mental strategy. The following are a few ways you can better cultivate your ability to let go.

Tips and Reflections for Letting Go

- When you identify an issue or problem that seems to stay with you, to follow you from task to task or from work to home, mentally hold on to it. Isolate the *nam* before the *toks* begin to multiply. Then after you isolate it and observe it, let it pass. And instead, purposefully refocus on what's happening in the moment.

- Once you commit to daily mindfulness training, intend to let go of every thought that arises. Let any distraction go, too. After all, it's a thought that sets distractions in motion. Let go of your desire to be fixated on any single thing in particular. Let go of your expectations about results. Let go of everything. Just be present.

- Use the quality of relaxation to help you let go of your thoughts. When you think, you create tension in your body. When you relax your body, you also relax your thoughts. Relax your body and allow a natural mental relaxation to follow. Then, use your focus on the experience of breathing to help you let go of thoughts and be in the moment—one breath at a time.

- As you begin to explore the nature of your thoughts, you will notice that some can be very difficult to let go of. Consider seeing these as opportunities to rewire your brain to let go more easily. Every time one of these difficult thoughts comes up, notice the thought is there and see if you can let it go or not.

PART III

Foundational Practices

So far, we've spent a significant amount of time covering techniques for being more mindful and effective in the workplace, as well as a number of mental strategies for cultivating qualities like patience, kindness, and joy. I hope by now you have been inspired to change some of your working habits as well as thought patterns and thereby created a little more mind space and effectiveness in your life.

But obviously mindfulness is about much more than work techniques and mental strategies. At its core, mindfulness is about going to the mental gym and moment by moment rewiring the neurological pathways of your brain. Mindfulness is a training. It is work, but a very pleasant kind of work.

Mindfulness training is an investment. It takes time. And it takes effort. And while many would argue they have no time for mindfulness training because they are busy, I see it very differently. Mindfulness training is increasingly important to me, the busier I get. The more things I need to do, the more time I train. That's my way of ensuring I can stay focused, calm, and effective and not let the busyness clutter my mind.

Now the time has come to introduce the actual mindfulness training to you. This part of the book is about training your mind by setting aside time for daily training.

In Chapters 2 and 3, I will introduce to you the two primary methods of mindfulness training: (1) sharp focus, which increases your general focus, clarity, and calmness, and thereby effectiveness in life, and (2) open awareness, which increases your self-awareness and insight into what makes you genuinely happy.

Chapter 4 provides the detailed, how-to guidance you need to systematically train both sharp focus and open awareness, and to put all the techniques and strategies of this book into a practice. Together, let's begin reshaping your life in ten minutes a day.

CHAPTER 2

Training Sharp Focus

Like many of us, Susanne was constantly busy. As a director of a large global French pharmaceutical company, her calendar was booked almost every day, from early morning to early evening. No day ever seemed to be long enough for her to do all that needed to be done.

In fact, her "to-do" list was more a repository for the things she couldn't finish than anything else. A result of her hardly being able to concentrate on one task long enough to finish it, the list itself grew and grew, becoming its own source of frustration.

While her own strategies for planning and organizing worked reasonably well, she kept finding herself stressed and overwhelmed. She tried every new time management course or productivity app, but none of them could help her feel in control.

Susanne needed to try something new. More than just a new strategy, she needed sharp focus. So rather than stick with her failing tactics and expect different results, Susanne turned to mindfulness training.

After a few months of regular practice, she began to notice a marked difference, saying, "I look at my calendar and tasks and I'm just as busy as before, but I don't feel the busyness in the same way. I am busy, but more relaxed and focused."

Mindfulness training—and focus training in particular—isn't about having fewer responsibilities. It's not about eliminating everyday busyness or becoming more organized. Rather, it is about seeing distractions for what they are and not letting them take control.

Sharp focus is the ability to concentrate on thoughts and tasks of your choice, without feeling the need to indulge each and every distraction that passes through your mind. Having this sort of mental clarity can help the busiest of us thrive, even in high-pressure environments filled with distractions.

For Susanne, such a focus meant the difference between feeling out of control or developing a true balance and stability in her life. In her own words, "It is as if I have more capacity to face the busyness and not get overwhelmed by it. I can keep things more in perspective. That has brought me more peace of mind and more enjoyment in my work and life."

And who of us couldn't use a little more balance and stability?

Who couldn't use a little more peace of mind?

Based on my experience, people who diligently train for ten minutes a day, five to seven days a week, observe significant improvements in their ability to concentrate in a relatively short time period. Third-party evaluations and internal surveys consistently show improvements averaging 15 percent in ability to maintain focus.[1]

Training your focus is simple, but not effortless. Our thoughts just aren't always easy to manage. Difficulties around training sharp focus can become their own sources of frustration. Even so, the work of training your focus can also be a source of great joy and inner calm if you let it. To do so, let go of your expectations. Feelings of frustration, calm, or even happiness are not indications of success in and of themselves. Success in training is the ability to manage your wandering mind with relaxation, focus, and clarity. It's being able to concentrate in the midst of distraction—being one second ahead of whatever might try to seize your attention.

The goal of this chapter is to explain how training sharp focus can help you master your attention. Together, we'll begin by exploring a simple process that facilitates focus training. Then we'll review the three qualities necessary for a high-performing, focused mind and finish with a review of the substantial benefits associated with training sharp focus.

The ABCD Method

Mindfulness training is not passive. It's an active intervention in your brain's neural network. For every moment you maintain focus, you create new "focus" neural connections and abilities. Thanks to neuroplasticity, the more you train, the stronger these neural connections and pathways become—and the easier it becomes to stay focused.

To facilitate focus training, we have distilled the process into a simple, four-point method with an easy-to-remember acronym: ABCD, see Figure 2.1. Each element of the method is described in detail below.

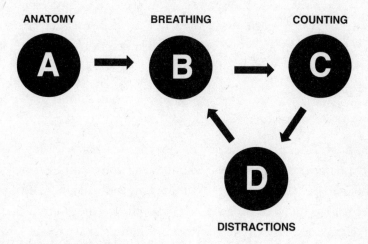

Figure 2.1 ABCD focus training.

Anatomy: Finding the Right Posture

It may seem strange to begin mental training with a discussion of anatomy, but it's well established through research that posture has a significant influence on our mental state.

When you train your mind, it's important—especially in the early stages—that your body not get in the way. To find a good posture during training, these guidelines will be very useful for you.

Steps to Sit Comfortably

- Sit on a chair with both feet planted firmly on the floor. Find balance. Don't lean back, forward, or to either side.
- Sit with your back straight, but relaxed. Sitting up straight will help you to stay awake and alert.
- Relax your body as much as you can. Pay special attention to your neck, shoulders, and arms—the places where many of us carry tension. Take time to release any tension you may feel. If it helps, roll your neck or move your shoulders up and down a few times. Also, take a deep breath and relax as you breathe out.
- Place your hands on your knees or in your lap.
- Close your eyes. If you start to doze off, open your eyes a little. Letting a small amount of light in activates your nervous system. If you opt to keep your eyes open, look down at the floor in front of you with a soft gaze.
- Breathe in and out through your nose.

You may find it helps to scan your body for tension, releasing it everywhere you notice it, for the first few minutes of your training—or as long as it takes to feel alert but relaxed. In this way, you will gradually develop a more relaxed body. And a more relaxed body lays the groundwork for a more relaxed mind, both prerequisites for training sharp focus.

With time, it gets easier and easier to be purposeful and intentional in your training. You will notice the warning signs earlier and be able to stay clear before drowsiness takes hold.

Once you're seated, comfortable, and relaxed, find an anchor for your attention.

Breathing: The Anchor for Attention

Have you ever been on a boat? Not a cruise ship, but something smaller, like a skiff or a sail boat?

It's impossible to stay in one spot—to stay focused—if your boat keeps floating away with every wave or gust of wind that hits you. To keep yourself from drifting off, you need to drop anchor.

An unfocused mind can be a little like an untethered boat: mean-dering, with no charted path, heading off course any chance it gets. To manage your wandering mind, you need an anchor for your attention. Breathing, the "B" of ABCD, can be that anchor in terms of practicing sharp focus.

And while, in theory, you could choose anything as an anchor, breathing has two important advantages. First, breathing stimulates the parasympathetic nervous system, enabling you to rest and relax better. (There's a reason why people say to "take a deep breath" when you're upset.) Second, breathing is always available. No matter where you are or where you go, your breath will be there with you. The following are guidelines for breathing.

Steps for Anchoring with Your Breath

- Focus your full attention on the experience of breathing. Be aware of how your stomach expands when you breathe in and contracts when you breathe out.
- If focusing on your belly doesn't feel natural, try observing your breathing at the nostrils. Pay attention to the air flowing in and out of your nose.
- Let the observation of your breath be neutral and effortless. You don't need to breathe deeply or slowly. You don't need to manipulate or change it. You don't have to get involved in it in any way. Observe it in the same way you would waves rolling in to beach. You don't try to control the waves—you just watch. While it can be challenging, neutral observation is very impor-tant as we go further into the training.

When your body and mind are relaxed and you anchor your focus on your breath, counting your breaths will help you stay on track.

Counting for Focus

Even when a boat is anchored at sea, there's a strong possibility that a rogue wave or quick storm will disturb what was otherwise calm.

Similarly, as you sit quietly and focus on your breathing, almost inevitably you will experience intrusive thoughts and distractions. Counting your breaths—the "C" of ABCD—can be a great way to stay focused.

Here are a few tips to help you use counting as a way to train and maintain sharp focus.

Counting to Stay on Track

- Breathe in. Breathe out. When you finish breathing out, count "one." A short and succinct mental count. Breathe in again, out again, and count "two." Carry on in the same way until you

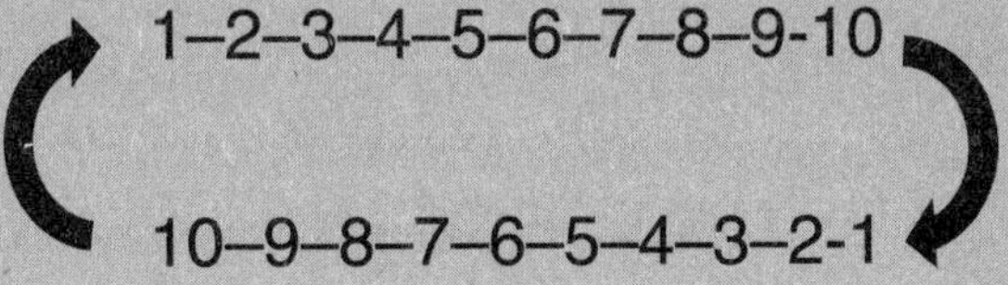

$$1–2–3–4–5–6–7–8–9–10$$
$$10–9–8–7–6–5–4–3–2–1$$

Figure 2.2 Counting your breaths.

  get to ten, then count backward to one. Repeat this cycle (see Figure 2.2).
- If you have trouble counting higher than three or seven without losing focus, don't worry. The point of counting is not to see how many times you get through the cycle; rather, it's a tool to help you maintain focus.
- If you suddenly find yourself at 37, you've been counting on autopilot and are not managing your attention. Start again at one. In the same way, if you find you've stopped counting altogether, simply start again at one.
- If you find thoughts sneaking in between numbers, that's a sign you're not fully focused on your breath. Sharpen your focus on your breath and give it your full attention, in a relaxed manner.

For most people, counting is a great help for training sharp focus, especially when they're just getting started. Still, some people find counting to be a distraction. If you're one of those people, drop the counting and just focus on your breath.

Count when it helps.

Don't count when it gets in the way.

As with many things in mindfulness training, it's best to keep the end goals in sight—a relaxed body and a calm mind. If counting, or any other specific tactic gets in the way, don't get upset. Instead, be grateful that you've recognized what doesn't work for you and see it as an opportunity to make your own training more effective.

The last element of the ABCD method looks specifically at dealing with distractions.

Distractions: Relax, Release, Return

Distractions are your best friends in focus training. Distractions are the ones telling you when you are off track.

What is a distraction? Basically anything that is not your breath is a distraction. And they can come from six sources: smell, taste, bodily sensations, sight, sounds, and the mind itself. Regardless of where the distraction comes from, the instructions for dealing with it are the same: *Relax, Release,* and *Return*.

Mastering Distractions

- Relax: When you perceive you are distracted by a thought, sound, or sensation, notice whether it creates any tension anywhere in your body. Try your best to release that tension. Relax. Recognize the fact that you have been distracted. It's really not the end of the world. Instead of getting frustrated or annoyed, think of that distraction as a good friend—one who gently reminds you that your attention has drifted. Treat every time you notice yourself being distracted as a moment to celebrate. After all, when you are aware that your mind has drifted, you are being mindful!

- Release: Release whatever distraction you may encounter, simply by redirecting your focus toward your breath. Your full focus can only be in one place at a time. If you choose your breath, the distraction is gradually released. Let go of the distraction gratefully, it helped you notice the fact that you had lost track of your breathing.

- Return: Once you have released the distraction and regained a sense of relaxation, come back to your breathing with renewed focus and awareness.

You'll likely find focus training is a continual back and forth between paying attention to your breathing and being distracted. Some days, there will be more distractions than focus. Other days, there will be more focus than distraction.

Remember, the objective is not to sit without distractions. If it were, none of us would succeed. The objective is to be aware of the fact that you're distracted and to acknowledge that you have the ability to regain your focus on your breath. It's the conscious placing of our attention that's critical to training sharp focus.

While training this, you are turbocharging your neural networks for when you go to work. You are training your mind to be more focused on the task at hand regardless of what it is, and at the same time to be aware when you are distracted, and redirecting your focus back to the chosen task. These two skills are extremely useful in any fast-paced, demanding work environment.

The Three Core Qualities of Mindfulness: Relaxation, Focus, and Clarity

In focus training, there are three essential qualities for a high-performing mind: relaxation, focus, and clarity. These three qualities apply to any situation in which we need to effectively manage our attention: when we need to be present with others, when we're working, and when we're training our mind.

These three qualities help us to perform at our best.

They give us an advantage over our distractions. They get us one second ahead.

These qualities are also antidotes to the three main challenges people experience in mindfulness training: tension, overactivity, and drowsiness. Tension can be overcome with relaxation, overactivity with focus, and drowsiness is no match for clarity. The following sections offer specific guidance for each of these methods.

Overcome Tension with Relaxation

Maybe your shoulders feel tense after work.

Or maybe you get stress headaches.

Regardless of how tension manifests itself, we have all been neurologically programmed to perform. Whether at work or at home, many of us are under a lot of pressure to get things done as quickly as possible. Constant pressure to perform creates deep neurological patterns of tension in our nervous systems.

When you practice mindfulness, you may find yourself caught up in this neurological "performance mode." It may seem almost unnatural to sit still, especially with so many tasks that need to be done. In the spirit of performance, you may push yourself to follow training instructions without truly understanding their greater purpose. But wanting to be "good at" mindfulness so you can get it over with—and assume the benefits of a high-performing mind as soon as possible—won't get you very far.

Sharp focus can only come from a relaxed mind. But with tension virtually ingrained in us, how do we cultivate relaxation effectively? Consider the following tips.

Cultivating Relaxation

- When you breathe in, scan your body to identify points where you are experiencing tension. When you breathe out, pay attention to that point and allow the tension to release.
- Let the tension be released with the breath. It may be necessary to repeat the exercise several times to be effective. Take as much time as needed with each tension point before moving on to the next point where you find tension.

- Keep in mind the following definition: "Relaxation is the absence of unnecessary effort." Scan your body for any unnecessary effort and gently let it go.
- Scan and release tension in your body for the first minute of your training or as long as it takes to increase your ability to be alert but relaxed. In this way you will gradually develop a more relaxed body and mind.

Remember, every time you relax, you create new neural connections—connections that make it easier for you to do it again. Also you develop "muscle memory" of what relaxation is—and how it can be triggered by a mental decision. With training you will gradually teach your muscles to relax on your call and that call can be made before delivering an important presentation, during a challenging meeting, or when you try to fall asleep at night. And a relaxed body and mind is the best foundation for developing greater focus.

Overcome Overactivity with Focus

A focused mind does not wander. A focused mind can stay focused on an object of choice. But sometimes our minds can be overactive, wandering in every possible direction or following every distraction that arises.

While some people are naturally more focused than others, everyone can increase their focus through training. And regardless of your best efforts, you'll likely find it challenging at times to stay focused on your breath. When you find your mind is overstimulated, take it as an opportunity to cultivate focus. To do so, follow one of these two strategies.

Cultivating Focus

- In many instances, the natural response to an excited mind is frustration, and the result is to try to force greater attention on your breath. Although applying such force may help you maintain focus, it will be exhausting and counterproductive to creating a calm and clear mind. The first response to an overactive and distracted mind is to *relax*.

- The alternative strategy for increasing focus is to actually let go of performance expectations. Let your breath hold your attention. Your breathing works by itself. Every in-breath is followed by an out-breath. Rest your full attention in this movement, effortlessly, as a neutral observer.

The ability to manage your focus is essential for anything you want to achieve in life. By following these two strategies over time, slowly you will create new neural connections, making relaxed alert focus the rule rather than the exception. This type of focused mind is the foundation for developing mental clarity, the last of the three essential qualities.

Overcome Drowsiness with Clarity

A drowsy mind can be just as challenging as an overactive mind. Even though it may seem like you've achieved one of the objectives of mindfulness training—you feel very calm and relaxed—drowsiness is not a beneficial state of mindfulness. Instead, drowsiness is experienced as a dark, foggy, and dull mind.

A mind with clarity, on the other hand, is fully awake. It's a mind that sees clearly and perceives the finest details, like a high-definition monitor. The following suggestions will help you maintain clarity as you practice training sharp focus.

Cultivating Clarity

- When you experience drowsiness, you need to arouse your attention and increase alertness. You can do this by sitting up a little straighter or taking an intentionally deep breath. You can also open your eyes, keeping them pointed downward toward the floor to minimize distractions.

- Another strategy to increase clarity is to arouse a deep sense of curiosity in the natural experience of breathing. Experience each breath as a new experience. Be curious about the subtle detail of your breath: Where do you notice it? How does it feel? What's it doing?
- When you first experience any sense of drowsiness, increase your alertness. Don't let the dullness take hold. Be purposeful and intentional in your training. With time, it gets easier. You will notice the warning signs earlier and be able to stay clear before drowsiness takes hold.

When you have a clear mind during your training, you see all of the details of your breathing. You also notice immediately when you get distracted. Similarly, when you have a clear mind in day-to-day life, you see details in other people's expressions, more easily reading their state of mind. You also begin to see the wealth of opportunities that lie in every challenge. By getting one second ahead of your automatic reactions, it allows you to see potential where before you saw limitations. This is why it's so important to be aware of the three challenges and the three qualities when doing your daily ABCD training.

How would your day-to-day life be different if you could handle each pressing and challenging situation with a mind that is relaxed, focused, and clear? By training the three qualities of relaxation, focus, and clarity, you'll be able to develop the ability—with a few simple breaths—to find a relaxed state with sharp focus and clarity of mind even in the most difficult situations. As David, a senior manager at a global American-based financial services company, described it, "Focus training has given me the ability to stay calm and clear minded even in the chaos of life."

Of course, mindfulness training is very personal in the sense that everyone experiences it differently. Even so, there are a few outcomes everyone can look forward to.

The Benefits of Focus Training

If you've already started training your focus, you may be wondering whether your experiences are the same as other people's experiences. In next few pages, I'll explore some common benefits that people experience, including improved focus, increased responsiveness, enhanced creativity, and greater happiness.

Improved Focus

Naturally, one of the main objectives of focus training is to improve your ability to focus. Although many people experience noticeable improvements in their overall effectiveness, ability to concentrate, and the quality of their sleep, some people question their progress based solely on how well—or poorly—they can focus on their breath during daily training.

This can be misleading.

Sometimes people feel like they're not making progress when, in fact, they are. This is especially true when people have unrealistic expectations or believe the purpose of the training is to *never* be distracted. But understand, just because your mind still wanders during your mindfulness training doesn't mean you aren't making progress.

You are.

When you start to train your focus, it naturally increases, as does the bandwidth of your attention. Once this happens, you begin to detect and discern things you never noticed before. You become aware of a whole new level of distractions that were always there, but were not in your field of awareness.

Ultimately, mindfulness training is not about being able to sit still and maintain focus on your breath. It's about improving your ability to focus on the most important facets of your life: your work, your coworkers, and your family. Most people notice the greatest impact in these areas after just a few weeks. Try to relax and enjoy the benefits you're experiencing—even if, in the beginning, this is just ten minutes of space, stillness, and peace in your life.

Increased Responsiveness Versus Reactiveness

There are many things in life that are beyond our control. We can't control the weather, or traffic, or the negative feedback we get from our boss. But we can control how we respond. This raises a couple of important questions for each of us to consider: Will we allow external circumstances and other people's actions to negatively impact us? Or, instead, will we turn it around and see it as a strength to not always react?

Creating a gap between stimulus and response gives us the freedom to answer these questions: to choose when and how *we* want to respond. This is the one-second difference between intentionally responding and instinctively reacting. It's the one-second advantage needed in critical decision-making. It's also the foundation for mental peace, happiness, and well-being.

The more you train your focus, the bigger the gap between input and impulsive reactions. As you go further in your training, you'll recognize thoughts before they fully come to your conscious awareness. You can then let them pass before they materialize. It's this ability that generates the powerful gap between stimulus and response. And in this way, we gain more control over our lives—we open the door for choice—and become less and less often the victims of circumstance.

Enhanced Creativity

Let's say you sit down to do your daily ten minutes of mindfulness training and you suddenly have the answer to a problem that's been weighing you down for weeks.

What do you do?

Do you open your eyes and scribble down your creative break-through? Or do you observe it, recognize it as a distraction, and have faith you will remember it when you finish your training?

Tough choice!

One of the truly amazing benefits of focus training is that when we reduce some of the clutter in our minds, creative ideas tend to bubble up to the surface. As we discussed in the technique on applying mindfulness to enhance creativity, there are many reasons why a more relaxed, focused, and clear mind generates more creative insights. But for now, as we look at ways to support effective focus training, it's important to let go of all distractions, even if that distraction seems like the greatest, most innovative idea you've ever had.

Why?

For two reasons. First, as you start training, you may find creative ideas pop up often. While it might be nice to engage all the wonderful thoughts that percolate during your quiet time, you won't be training your mind. Sitting and thinking about big ideas for ten minutes is not the same as training your focus. Instead, regardless of how brilliant an idea may seem in the moment, train yourself to meet distractions by returning your focus to your breath.

The second reason is that it's important to develop faith in the process. One of the key benefits of focus training is improved memory. Have faith that, if the idea is really that good, it will come back when you've finished your training. It might even return in sharper focus. As Kathryn, a stand-up comedian in Australia, shared, "When I don't chase after the ideas during my training and just let them go and continue to focus on my breath, I find after the training, the ideas come back with greater clarity. It's been a wonderful way to increase calm and simultaneously create more mental space for really great ideas."

Greater Peace and Happiness

Imagine if you had a greater ability to focus in a relaxed way, with a clearer, less reactive mind. What would that do to your happiness and overall sense of well-being?

Some of the most common outcomes of focus training are that people find themselves to be less stressed, calmer, and able to get more enjoyment out of life. Together, that can be a pretty powerful recipe for well-being and happiness.

In evaluating happiness, your own experience is by far the best measure. Pay attention to your own levels of happiness as you dive into your training. Ask those close to you if they notice a difference in you. Sometimes it's easier for other people to see changes before you notice them in yourself.

Besides subjective self-evaluation, research strongly supports the relationship between increased focus and greater happiness. Matthew Killingsworth and Daniel Gilbert, researchers from Harvard University, found that when the mind wanders—even to pleasant thoughts—our subjective experience of happiness doesn't increase. They summarized their findings by writing, "The human mind is a wandering mind, and a wandering mind is not the happiest mind. The ability to think about what is not happening right now is a cognitive ability that has emotional costs."[2]

In short, when we're not focused and present with what is happening right now, when we let our minds wander, we're less happy. Conversely, the same research showed that a focused mind—defined as a mind that is present with what is happening in any given moment—is happier than a mind wandering to positive past or future events.[3]

Science is increasingly coming to conclusions similar to those that mindfulness masters have described for thousands of years. In the mindfulness tradition, it's well known that a focused mind leads directly to greater mental satisfaction. When the mind is fully focused, it becomes an inexhaustible source of joy and inner peace.

From Sharp Focus to Open Awareness

When we manage to let go of our expectations, focus training can be very peaceful and rewarding. It's the starting point for developing a high-performing mind—one that's relaxed, focused, and clear both during training and in day-to-day life.

But mindfulness doesn't stop here.

In training open awareness, as explored in the next chapter, you go a step further. During open awareness training, a sharpened focus helps generate insight into both the nature of the mind and how its performance can be optimized. With open awareness training, you develop a panoramic view that helps you see yourself, others, and every situation more objectively—allowing you to decide who and what gets your attention, and who and what does not.

CHAPTER 3

Training Open Awareness

Ribur Rinpoche was a highly respected mindfulness master from Tibet. At the age of 36, he was thrown into a Chinese prison because of his Buddhist associations.

For the next 17 years, he was tortured every day.

In the face of this incessant brutality, most people would break down. Most people would harden their hearts toward their attackers. Not knowing if or when they would be released, if or when they would be tortured again, or if they would live to see the next day, most people would very likely sink into despair.

Rinpoche was an exception to that rule.

While in captivity, Rinpoche continued to practice the mindfulness training that he had learned over many years. Although his body was a victim of his captors, his mind was at ease.

Amazingly, after he was released, he still had the same strength and joy for life as when he was taken captive. Perhaps even more incredible, he came out of prison with a deep empathy for the guards who had been forced to torture him. Having been on the receiving end of their violence, he had great compassion for the suffering they must have endured in inflicting it.

How is it that a person could endure such suffering, yet come out on the other side filled with joy and compassion for his torturers?

The answer: open awareness.

Open awareness is the ability to observe your mind. It is a training in becoming familiar with the workings of the mind and how that causes us to experience challenges in life. Open awareness helps you not be a victim of circumstance—only able to react automatically to situations as they develop. Open awareness involves training for a new kind of relationship with your thoughts and the world around you. It engenders a certain clarity in the mind, allowing you to stay one second ahead of your reactions, regardless of the situation. With open awareness, autopilot is no longer the default response mechanism. Instead, it catalyzes the ability to relate to the events in your mind, bringing a whole new sense of clarity and direction into your life and work.

Ribur Rinpoche is just one example of the many people who have faced extreme hardship and come out stronger for the experience. These people are living proof that it's not the circumstances themselves that create our problems; rather, it's our way of relating to them.

This, however, is no easy realization. And it doesn't happen overnight. It would be great if we could simply be above reacting to all the challenges we face in life. Unfortunately, it just isn't that easy or convenient. We can't simply reprogram all of our thought processes just by telling ourselves to think differently. There is no button to push or switch to flip that will magically allow us to disregard our biases, look beyond our frustrations, or let go of our pain.

This is why open awareness training is so valuable.

Training open awareness provides you with the opportunity to experience, with a depth of understanding, that your thoughts are the root cause of your problems.

While the previous chapter discussed the importance of developing sharp focus, focus alone can be blind. The mind can tempt focus to follow any distraction that happens to be more interesting than breathing, whether a shopping list, an e-mail, or an upcoming vacation. Open awareness gives sharp focus direction and intentionality. Together, sharp focus *and* open awareness can help you spend your time, energy, and attention mindfully, ultimately increasing your effectiveness in life and work. Together, sharp focus *and* open awareness can give you that one-second advantage, potentially the difference between just getting by or actually getting ahead.

This chapter aspires to lead you further down the path toward gaining that extra one second between an automatic thought and a deliberate response. To do so, I'll take a look at the basics of training open awareness and some of its specific insights, as well as what you stand to gain through your efforts.

The Choice Is Yours

Imagine sitting down at your computer during a busy day at work. You've been running between back-to-back meetings and barely had enough time to catch your breath, let alone eat lunch. You finally feel like you have a minute to concentrate on your work.

But suddenly a series of e-mails hits your inbox—five, eight, fifteen—a growing avalanche of questions and requests. You feel the pressure start to build as you think about all of the things you already have to do. And now this, a new set of distractions striking without warning.

You alternate back and forth between your original task and this deluge of new e-mails, doing your best to multitask, but feeling as though you're hardly making progress.

Probably not that much of a stretch for many of us, right?

Now, instead of the new set of distractions consuming you, imagine being aware of them, but not distracted. Imagine that instead of immediately reacting to each new e-mail as it chimes in your inbox, you have a choice in how to respond. Seeing that the e-mails are not urgent, you simply observe them neutrally, aware that they exist, and keep your attention focused on the task at hand.

Open awareness isn't about minimizing the number of distractions in your life. On the contrary, it's about seeing those distractions as precisely what they are and choosing which ones deserve your attention. The essence of open awareness training is observing your thoughts, senses, emotions and tasks in a neutral way—like a mental observatory. In this way, focus and awareness are closely linked. When you train your focus, as discussed in the previous chapter, you sharpen your mental telescope. You learn to look closely at objects or experiences of your choice, like your breathing. When training open awareness, you point your telescope toward the inner workings of your mind and observe what is happening in order to gain insight into your own experience. Training open awareness can be a source of both greater mental freedom and self-understanding.

Open Awareness Training

How many seconds of your day are lost to worry or stress or to the illusion you can multitask? How many moments are wasted thinking about things you can't change? For many of us, the answer to questions like these is "too many."

Consider George, a team leader at a large American manufacturing company. George was once at the mercy of his thoughts, getting caught up in each and every thought that came into his mind.

If you have started training, you will likely have a sense of the sheer number of thoughts you experience in just ten minutes of focusing on your breath. Now, imagine addressing each and every thought you have all day, every day. That was George.

After training open awareness, George came away with some powerful insights into his own thought patterns and mental activities: "I now realize I don't have to think about every thought that comes into my head. As strange as it sounds, it is now clear to me that some of my thoughts are actually not worth thinking about and I am better off letting them go."

But open awareness is not just about throwing unhelpful thoughts into an "ignore" pile. For George, training open awareness changed his entire relationship with his thoughts. As he put it, "It's incredibly useful to have the ability to step back from my thoughts and give myself a little time and space to choose whether and how I want to respond." Taking just one second to step back before reacting can end up saving you many, many minutes and hours of needless worry and unproductive work habits.

Of course, it's not easy to change your way of thinking and looking at the world. Thankfully, there is simple process you can use to rewire your mind.

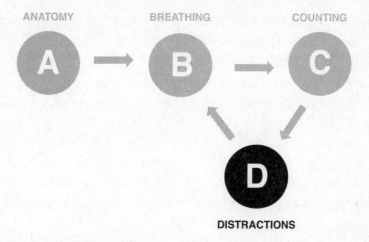

Figure 3.1 Open awareness training.

When training open awareness, it isn't your breathing that's the anchor for your attention, like with sharp focus, but your distractions (see Figure 3.1).

It begins with the basic ABCD model. This is to ensure your mind is calm, clear, and focused. Once you have developed a sufficient level of focus, you open your awareness and become an observer of your own experiences. The specific guidelines for open awareness training are as follows.

Steps to Train Open Awareness

- As in focus training, start by sitting comfortably, as described under the guidance in the "A" for Anatomy.
- For a minute or two, direct your full attention toward your breathing, like in the focus training. Allow your mind to stabilize and settle. Count your breaths if it helps you let go of distractions. Check off one by one whether your mind has the three core qualities of relaxation, focus, and clarity.
- When you've reached some level of these qualities, you can begin to open your awareness.
- Let go of the attention on your breathing and open up to whatever may arise. When the first distraction attracts your

attention—a sound, thought, physical sensation, or anything else—direct your full attention to it and use it as an anchor for your awareness.

- Observe the distraction neutrally, just as you did with your breathing. Don't think about it. Don't engage in it. Don't try to make it stay or go away. Simply observe it. If it helps, imagine observing the distractions as if they were waves on the beach.

- Notice when the distraction comes into focus. Notice that it's there. Notice when at some point it disappears or changes to something else.

- When a distraction disappears, you open up and are ready to receive the next one in the same way. If a distraction changes into something else, you follow the transformation neutrally.

- If at any point you find you're confused or overwhelmed by your distractions, pause, relax, release the distractions, and return your focus to your breath. After a few moments, when you've stabilized your focus, let go of your breathing and open your awareness again.

- At any time, you can always come back to the anchor and simply focus on your breath. Be prepared that you may need to come back to your breath again and again throughout your training to ensure you're not getting carried away by thoughts and distractions.

- If it's difficult to have a neutral approach to the distraction, that is, if you notice you start to engage with it, it can be helpful to give it a short mental label. For example, if a thought arises about something you need to buy, you can label it "shopping" and observe the experience of the thought without thinking about what it is and where you will get it. You can also use even simpler labels such as "thought," "sensation," and "feeling," without qualifiers.

While the instructions are simple, the challenge for many is observing thoughts, feelings, sensations, and emotions neutrally without engaging. In fact, many find training open awareness difficult, especially in the beginning.

But the mental strength and freedom you develop by training open awareness cannot be overstated. That one second you gain between having a thought and thinking about it can be the difference between having pain and being in pain, feeling anger and being angry, or having anxiety and being anxious. In short, the second you gain in open awareness training can change how you experience the world and respond to everything in life.

The ability to *observe* your thoughts and experiences instead of *being* your thoughts and experiences not only results in more effectiveness and mental peace but also preserves your energy. After all, thinking too much is the core cause of mental exhaustion.

Use open awareness as a basis for your training for a couple of weeks as you develop your ability to be a neutral observer of your thoughts and experiences. When you feel able to respond to distractions deliberately rather than react automatically, you can move to the next level of open awareness training that includes the three insights outlined below.

The Three Insights

The three insights of open awareness—Everything Changes, Happiness Is a Choice, and Everything Is Potential—are basic facts of life. They relate to the nature of change, the sources of our unhappiness, and the nature of our own self. When we understand them, they can transform both the way we live and the way we face challenges in our lives.

Insight #1: Everything Changes

We've all experienced difficult situations in life. This could be anything from losing a job, to worrying about a health problem, to having a child in distress. Situations that frustrate us, make us angry, or cause upset are truly challenging, often leading to distressing or otherwise unhelpful thoughts.

Fortunately, no one situation is permanent. Change is inevitable.

Rationally, we understand that even the most frustrating situation will eventually change. Even so, the mind has a tendency to hold on to difficult situations as if they will always be there.

The first insight of open awareness is about developing an instinctive understanding that everything changes, that everything is transitory. Everything.

The more you come to grasp, in a meaningful way, the fact that everything changes, the easier it becomes to deal with negative things, because you know they will change. You will also place a higher value on the positive things you experience, appreciating them more while they last. In your training, and in life, when observing your distractions, regardless of what they are, ask yourself the following questions:

- Is there anything you experience that is unchanging?
- Is there a thought that never goes away?
- Is there anything solid and static, or is it all a process?

Ask yourself these questions again and again. What do you find? Many reach a deep and instinctive recognition of the fact that everything changes. Any distraction that occurs goes away with time. Since unpleasant things disappear, any resistance is a waste of energy. On the flip side, pleasant things also disappear, making any attachment a similar waste of energy.

How often have you found yourself dwelling on the unpleasant? Now, imagine how much more time and energy you can put toward being an effective leader, partner, parent, or friend just because you took one second to step back and see the truth of the insight that everything changes.

The more you train yourself to see everything as changing, the easier it becomes to manage life's difficult situations—and appreciate life's beauty while it lasts. When you are no longer attached to things you like or resistant to things you dislike, you develop greater freedom.

Insight #2: Happiness Is a Choice

Imagine two identical cars are stopped beside each other on the highway, both caught in the same traffic jam. Both drivers are headed to the same meeting. While the first driver is sitting peacefully, enjoying the morning sunshine and the quiet in his car, the second driver is consumed with anger and frustration, and everyone and everything seems to be in his way.

What's the difference between the two? Objectively, if the traffic jam were the true source of frustration, shouldn't both drivers be blaring their horns at the creeping cars ahead of them?

The difference is not in the situation itself; rather, it's in the drivers.

The two drivers are relating to the exact same situation in two very different ways. One driver accepts the fact that he can't move any faster than the flow of traffic. Instead of wasting energy on anger and frustration, he uses the time to enjoy a well-earned break. The second driver, however, is his own worst enemy. From his seat behind the wheel, he creates a mental drama that doesn't bring him any closer to his destination, all while taxing his energy, health, and well-being.

Similarly, the situations we experience don't cause frustration or anger on their own. Rather, it's the way we relate to our surroundings that creates the problems we perceive in life. Regardless of external circumstances, we are the source of our own happiness or frustration. By changing our worldview, we have the potential to free ourselves from the problems we create. When you observe your distractions, ask yourself:

- Does this thought contribute to my happiness or my suffering?
- Is this thought helpful in terms of nurturing who I want to be and what I want to do in life?
- Does this help me make a positive difference for other people?

All your thoughts influence you, if you let them. But it can be liberating to realize the power you have to change your perspective on everything you experience. Through neutrally observing your thoughts, you will find some create stress, some create anger, and perhaps others generate frustration. Being aware of the kind of influence your thoughts wield can help you determine which are worth your time and which you might want to let go. And by training yourself to change how you view your thoughts, you change your experience of life. Open awareness is the first step to be able to do that.

There is a Cherokee legend of an old man sitting under a tree with his grandchildren telling them about life. "We all have two wolves inside us. One is bad and feels anger, jealousy, envy, falsehoods, and arrogance. The other is good and feels love, empathy, honesty, generosity, and humility. The two wolves constantly fight each other."

One of the grandchildren asks, "But which one wins?"

"The one you feed," the old man answers.

Open awareness is the prerequisite for seeing the fighting wolves inside you. And it is the prerequisite for feeding the one you prefer.

Insight #3: Everything Is Potential

Over the past 30 years, psychologists and neurologists have searched for the brain's control center: the place where the orders come from, the center of our true "self." Despite there being billions of neurons in the brain, no control center has been identified as the essence of an individual or a self.

From a scientific point of view, we appear to be an amazing collection of extremely complex systems and processes. And despite no control center existing, we are neurologically disposed toward the illusion of having an inherently existing self. We tend to experience ourselves as clearly defined, fixed entities with specific characteristics and properties. The greater the sense of a self, the bigger the target when others say or do something we don't like. The more we come to appreciate that we are not as simply and clearly defined as we think, the less vulnerable we become.

To explore this idea further, reflect on your own experience so far with open awareness training. When you're observing your thoughts, who is it that's doing the observation? If you're not your thoughts, then who exactly are you? Take some time to think about these questions and consider the ramifications.

This doesn't mean you don't exist. Rather, it means you don't exist in the way you think you do. If this sounds strange, then test it out for yourself. When you're training open awareness and you notice a sensation somewhere in your body, see if you can pinpoint who is having the sensation. At some point, you'll discover what many people have realized—it's impossible to find who exactly is experiencing the sensation. Instead, you'll find a lot of processes. There will be thoughts, feelings, perceptions, and sounds, but you won't be able to localize the owner of the sensation. The logical conclusion: you're not as clearly defined as you thought.

This is good news. If there's no specific owner of any experience, then it opens up a world of possibilities. The myriad distractions we're faced with daily transform from petty nuisances into possibilities.

Everything is potential.

The insight that everything is potential and that there is no solid, isolated self means we can redefine ourselves. We can break free of our own limited definitions of ourselves and others. New possibilities open up in every situation we encounter. Nothing is fixed. We have the choice to define all people and all situations based on our perspectives, however narrow or expansive they may be. When everything is potential, it offers each and every one of us an abundance of opportunities and positive outcomes.

What Do You Stand to Gain?

Training open awareness has been crucial for my own life—in my personal life, but especially my professional life. The three insights have helped me see my potential and be truly creative as an entrepreneur and leader. They've helped me to see potential and opportunities where others didn't. And they have helped me let go of my concerns about success, money, or conflicts. They've helped me be more present and handle difficult situations with greater clarity. And like Jacob, the overwhelmed manager described at the beginning of Chapter 1, they've allowed me to get one second ahead of distractions or negative thoughts.

While no two people will have exactly the same experience, thousands of people in our programs report common outcomes of open awareness training: enhanced mental capacity, improved relationship with thoughts, and more compassion for self and others.

Enhanced Mental Capacity

Picture yourself sitting down to write an important e-mail. While you're composing your e-mail, thoughts about playing golf this weekend or some things you need to buy on the way home pop up in your head.

If you allow your mind to engage these distractions, that e-mail will take much longer to write and probably not reflect your best effort. While your mind can be powerful, it can also be your worst enemy. When it holds on to things—either positive or negative—it can create its own clutter. All of us waste a lot of time and mental energy getting involved in distractions that are not helpful to us. In these situations, quite often, our mind is on autopilot and we're not in control of our thoughts.

But with open awareness training, you become more aware of distractions, while not giving them your attention. The end result is greater mental capacity to do the things you need to do, leaving you more time for yourself or other important people in your life.

Improved Relationship with Thoughts

The more we look at our thoughts, the more we find them to be a circus of random, repetitive, and often irrelevant fragments of memories, hopes, and passing experiences. Just because something passes through our mind doesn't mean it's relevant or true. Let your thoughts be thoughts without getting involved in them and without holding on.

Your thoughts are not you.

You are not your thoughts.

Imagine your mind is clear and pure like the sky. If your mind is the sky, your thoughts are the clouds. They pass through, occurring without anyone creating them and disappearing without anyone taking them away. There will be days when you feel your training is like a cloudless sky, clear and crisp, free of thoughts and distractions. But other days, you feel like your mind is filled with clouds, some of them dark and stormy. On those days, imagine elevating until you're above the clouds, where the sky is still clear and pure.

When you train open awareness, you develop the ability to lift yourself above the many distractions in life—above the dark clouds, to where the sky is still clear. Such a shift in perspective can nurture a wholly new relationship with your thoughts. They become passing clouds. While they may sometimes be relevant, they more often clutter your view and hamper your productivity.

More Compassion for Self and Others

Most people want to make a positive difference in the lives of others. When we are busy and overwhelmed, or under pressure and stressed, it is markedly more difficult to be considerate of other people's needs. It is for good reasons that the Chinese word for busyness consists of the two symbols, one for the word "killing" and the other the word "heart" (see Figure 3.2).

The mental stillness and peace that open awareness training help us see things more clearly in the moment, as well as focus on what is important. As a result of training, many people experience an increase in compassion for themselves and others.

Mindfulness and an ethical life are closely connected. On the one hand, it's almost impossible to train mindfulness if you're not in harmony with your surroundings. On the other hand, you are less likely to create disharmony when you are mindful.

Imagine practicing mindfulness immediately after an argument with someone. Your mind will likely be simmering with analyses of the situation. It may be very hard to focus and be openly aware. Mindfulness training is very difficult if you are weighed down by negative thoughts and emotions.

The more you train mindfulness, the less you'll be weighed down in negative thoughts and emotions. The reason is simple: you'll have greater awareness of your thoughts, words, actions, and surroundings. By extension, you'll become more aware of how your words and actions affect others. Naturally, this encourages more constructive relationships. More constructive relationships, in turn, result in greater mental peace. It then becomes easier to make helpful choices in your life, rather than ones that are harmful to yourself or others.

KILLING   HEART

Figure 3.2 The Chinese symbol for busyness.

Mindfulness helps us help other people. And the more we help others to be happier, the better our mindfulness becomes.

Mindfulness for Life

For me, mindfulness training is a core component of my day. It's time that's mine alone. In those moments, I am preparing my mind to handle a busy day as a father, partner, and leader of an international organization.

By training my focus—as discussed in the previous chapter—I get the benefits of being fully present with other people and my tasks. It helps me be relaxed, disciplined, and have a calm, clear mind, even when challenges arise.

Through training open awareness, I gain the ability to reduce unnecessary noise from the outer world, as well as my own mind. I see my thoughts and surroundings with greater insight. Situations often appear less complex, making even the most difficult problems easier to address.

While the time I spend training is invaluable, I don't just measure my success by the quality of my sessions. The most important evaluation of the effectiveness of my mindfulness training is by looking at the impact it has on the rest of my life: my compassion, focus, and presence with others. In the final part of the book, we'll look at how best to carry mindfulness training forward by practicing ten minutes a day.

CHAPTER 4

Mastering Your Life—Next Steps

Congratulations.

If you've made it this far, it means you've already experienced at least some of the many benefits of mindfulness. Maybe you've improved specific workplace skills like handling e-mail and managing meetings. Or maybe you've noticed an overall increase in efficiency and productivity. As a result, you've likely gained that one-second advantage identified in Chapter 1: that one-second gap between distractions and decisions that offers the opportunity to increase control and improve performance.

Now you're looking to expand the benefits of an increased sense of presence to the other facets of your life—to your community, your home, your family, and your friends. Although this book is primarily aimed at incorporating mindfulness into a work context, your work life and your private life are interconnected. Much like training your mind to better focus has an impact on your effectiveness at work, so too will it have an effect on your presence and well-being at home.

But patience is needed along the way. Mindfulness training takes time. There is no easy path leading to mindfulness. There are no step-by-step manuals or "cookbooks" that can take you there. You wouldn't expect to learn to fly a plane by reading a book about airplanes, right? Well, learning mindfulness is no different from any other skill that involves both mental and physical coordination.

We all have many projects in our lives: building a great career, having a strong family, being in good physical shape. However, mindfulness training is *not* just another project in the procession of these life projects. The minutes that you sit training your focus or awareness may be the only few minutes of the day that are really yours. Allow yourself to rest in these precious moments. It's your time. It's your mind.

It's your life.

Therefore, this chapter of the book is about you. It's about setting aside time for your daily mindfulness training and making it a consistent, harmonious facet of your life. The first part of the chapter briefly revisits The Matrix of Mental Effectiveness first identified in Chapter 1. This is followed by basic guidelines for structuring your daily training sessions and a detailed section on creating a self-guided training program. The chapter then ends with a brief look at how best to bring mindfulness into an organization.

Before we start, please remember that whatever you do in life, you always have the potential to do it with mindfulness. The following instructions are simple and clear. It's up to you, however, to decide whether to make something out of them or not.

Focused Awareness: Revisiting the Matrix

As we learned in Chapters 1, 2, and 3, there are two basic aspects to mindfulness training: (1) sharp focus, which is the force of concentration that enables you to keep your attention on your object of choice, and (2) open awareness, which is the introspective activity that tells you when your focus has wandered off into distractions.

Being the master of your mind—and your life—requires a combination of both focus and awareness. When joined, focus and awareness form the foundation for mental effectiveness and transform your mind into a highly efficient tool. This relationship is more easily understood when visually presented in The Matrix of Mental Effectiveness (see Figure 4.1), which was first described in Chapter 1.

Within the matrix, the vertical axis represents the continuum between being completely distracted to being sharply focused. When you're positioned near the top of the axis, your attention is focused solely on the task at hand and you recognize that most distractions can be set aside. Once it's been trained, this focus can be maintained for a

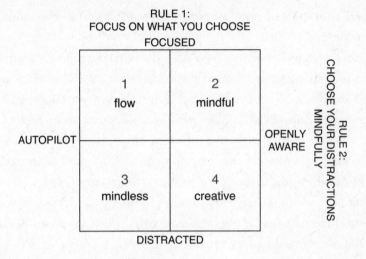

RULE 1:
FOCUS ON WHAT YOU CHOOSE
FOCUSED

1 flow	2 mindful
3 mindless	4 creative

AUTOPILOT

OPENLY AWARE

RULE 2:
CHOOSE YOUR DISTRACTIONS
MINDFULLY

DISTRACTED

Figure 4.1 The Matrix of Mental Effectiveness.

long time without difficulty. To learn more about specifically training sharp focus, I encourage you to read or review Chapter 2.

Moving left to right, the horizontal axis represents the continuum between being on autopilot—or acting on habitual patterns—to being openly aware. This open awareness provides you with the ability to have greater wisdom in terms of where best to place your focus. When this type of awareness develops, it naturally lets you see things from a calmer, more relative perspective. Situations that would normally cause you distress become easier because you don't engage so readily with difficult and unnecessary thoughts. To learn more about training open awareness, flip back to the previous chapter. In it, you'll find detailed instructions for developing the ability to observe your thoughts and feelings.

As you can see, the intersection of these two attributes occurs in the upper right quadrant. When you're in quadrant two, you're better able to manage your thoughts and overcome your habitual patterns. This means you have the ability to choose both how to respond to whatever you experience and where to place your precious attention. This enables you to be fully present with the people around you and what you're doing minute to minute. Through systematic mindfulness training, we all have the potential to do this in each and every moment of our lives.

This, in essence, is how you get *one second ahead* in work and in all aspects of life.

With dedicated training, you'll find yourself spending more and more time in quadrant two. Fortunately, for every moment you're in this quadrant, you generate neural connections in your brain that make it easier for you to be both focused and aware. Mindfulness is an active intervention that changes the neural networks in your brain. It simplifies the patterns of your thoughts and reactions. This makes you better at responding, rather than reacting, to everyday events and more capable of directly facing challenging circumstances. As you work to develop these new neural connections, you'll likely confront questions about how best to transform your training into a regular habit.

How, When, Where

When most people start a more regulated or formal mindfulness training program, they typically ask themselves a few practical questions: How long and how often should I train? When should I train? Where should I train?

In reality, there are many different answers to these questions depending on who you ask, your circumstances, and your objectives for training. The following are some basic guidelines intended to help you plan and structure your daily mindfulness training sessions.

How Long and How Often to Train

In my experience of guiding many people from a wide range of cultures, a minimum of ten minutes a day of mindfulness training ensures good results. As you gradually develop, you can increase the duration as much as you like. The more you do it, the more you'll get out of it. Just like with physical exercise, more time spent training equates to greater outcomes.

To be clear, however, the quality of your training time is more important than how long it takes. The critical factor for success is how focused and committed you are during your training. A good session for ten minutes is appreciably better than a half-hearted session for 20 minutes.

In terms of frequency, I recommend you set aside time every day to practice. Daily training is the best way to get results. When you do it every day, it will become a habit. The intensity of your training will improve, and your progress will be more tangible. Seven short daily sessions are preferable to one weekly session, so avoid letting your training become a weekend-only project.

In this sense, discipline is a big help. Much like the fact that a pot of water exposed to random or intermittent heat will never boil, occasional or random mindfulness training won't produce the desired results. To strengthen neural connections and build new neural networks, you need to train your mind consistently.

This may be the most difficult hurdle to overcome in getting started. Likely, one of the most pressing issues you face is having enough time in an already busy day. But consider your motivation for enhancing your mental fitness. What benefits would make the investment of ten minutes a day worthwhile to you? Better sleep? Better health? Greater empathy for family and friends?

See mindfulness training as the time you give to yourself without any conditions. See it as the time you give to yourself to develop a happier life. See it as the time you give to yourself in order to be able to care more for the ones you love. Then pay attention to how much you automatically react to events versus how often you're able to pause and choose your response. In my experience, people who commit to ten minutes of daily training start to notice a change in their ability to respond within a few weeks.

Before you begin your daily practice, remember your motivation and set intentions for your training. Then keep in mind that previous participants have said that after a few weeks of practice, although their time to tackle life's tasks is technically less, regular training creates a feeling of having more space and more time—even in the middle of a hectic day.

When to Train

We're all different. Some of us are morning people, some of us are night owls. Some of us like to eat dinner early, some late. Some of us like to take naps, some of us prefer an extended night of sleep. Similarly, we all have different preferences when it comes to the best time for mindfulness training.

But in my experience, the morning is a good time for most people. The mind is fresh, and therefore you get more out of the training. In addition, when you spend ten minutes at the start of the day to consciously be focused and aware, it has a strong influence on the rest of the day. Many people will say they don't have ten minutes to spare in the morning. The simple solution is to set your alarm clock 15 minutes earlier than usual. This gives you a couple of minutes to rise and gather yourself before you settle into your ten minutes of breathing, counting, or sensing. Doing so also means you won't have to crowd or bump the rest of your morning activities.

I get up before the rest of the family wakes up. There's an amazing calm at that time of the morning, which supports my training and energizes me for the rest of the day.

If you don't think that the morning is a good time for you, then find a time in the afternoon or evening that works better. What matters most is that you establish a fixed time so that your training becomes a habit after a few weeks.

Where to Train

The right place for mindfulness training is in your own head. You don't need a physical place that is completely quiet and harmonious. Mindfulness training is not religious or spiritual. It doesn't need to be practiced in clean, silent places. Rather, it's a state of mind that we can train and apply in any situation: while standing in line at the supermarket, while stuck in a traffic jam, while washing dishes, or while mowing the lawn. What's important is that you create calm and harmony within yourself.

With that said, when undertaking a formal training program, it is a good idea to find a regular place at home to practice. It can be a corner in your living room or your bedroom. It can be a sunny spot in a reading nook or a shadowy space in the basement. It can be anywhere you believe is conducive to quality training. A perfect, isolated spot with no distractions is rare, so be practical. Regardless of where you sit, you'll be able to hear sounds. That's okay. But try to choose a location that gives you the fewest distractions and allows you the space to comfortably assume and maintain the correct body posture, which is the physical foundation for successful training.

As a quick reminder, the correct body posture for mindfulness training incorporates five points: a grounded balance; a straight back; relaxed shoulders, arms, and neck; resting hands; and closed eyes. To help you determine your best location for training, let's take a closer look at each of these points.

- Grounded Balance: Make sure your training spot offers a firm connection with the ground beneath you. If you sit on a chair, can you place both feet comfortably on the ground? If you sit on the ground, do you have the space to sit cross-legged or in another balanced, comfortable posture? It's much easier to relax if you don't need to fight gravity to relax.
- A Straight Back: If you sit on a chair or sofa, make sure you can do so with a straight back. If it's a recliner or some other type of furniture that tempts you to lean back, you'll be more prone to becoming sleepy during training.
- Relaxed Shoulders, Arms, and Neck: Does your spot provide the space necessary to relax your shoulders and arms? Can you roll your shoulders up and back? Can you stretch your arms. Often, some stretching can help you relax and find your natural resting point at the beginning of training.
- Resting Hands: Is it easy to place your hands somewhere comfortable? Two good places are on the knees or in the lap, which means you don't want to be too close to a table, desk, or some other piece of furniture that may obstruct your hand placement.
- Closed Eyes: Some people feel vulnerable when they keep their eyes closed for an extended period of time. Does your chosen spot offer the sense of security and comfort necessary to keep your eyes closed or just barely open?

Any place you choose for your daily practice should offer you the space and comfort to incorporate all five of these points into your training. Now that you understand the basics of how, when, and where to do your training, let's examine a detailed framework for creating a personalized mindfulness program that will get you on the path to reshaping your life—and getting one second ahead—in just ten minutes a day.

Self-Directed Mindfulness Program

Mindfulness is not just a theory. Mindfulness is training. And as with any training, you won't achieve results without effort. Mindfulness training methods have been developed and practiced over thousands of years, so there's a logical progression in the training. When you follow the instructions in the right order, you'll achieve the best results in a shorter time. The following are the most basic guidelines for a ten-week self-directed training program. Each week you:

- Undertake ten minutes of sharp focus or open awareness training on a daily basis;
- select a mental strategy from Part II; and
- select one or two workplace techniques from Part I.

It doesn't sound too difficult, right? Integrating elements of the program one step at a time is the best way to realize results. You'll be doing ten minutes of daily practice, and each week focuses on one foundational practice from Part III, a new mental strategy from Part II, and your choice of workplace techniques from Part I. Table 4.1 presents an overview of a ten-week program that follows the traditional and logical progression of mindfulness training using sharp focus and open awareness training.

This program begins with focus training because it's the foundation for all the other elements. Only after you've developed a substantial level of focus—typically after four to five weeks of daily training—should you move on to awareness training. After the ten weeks, you'll have experienced both types of training and can choose the one you prefer.

Table 4.1 Self-guided training matrix

	Self-Guided Training for 10 Minutes per Day			Choose One Technique to Adopt for Week 4 and Beyond	
Week	Foundational Practice	Quality/Insight	Mental Strategy	Workplace Techniques	
1	Focus Training	No Quality/ Insight at Level 1	No Mental Strategy		
2	Focus Training	Relaxation	No Mental Strategy	E-mail	Mental Energy
3	Focus Training	Relaxation & Focus	Presence	Meetings	Sleep
4	Focus Training	Relaxation & Focus & Clarity	Patience	Goals	Eating & Energy
5	Focus Training	Relaxation & Focus & Clarity	Kindness	Priorities	Activity & Energy
6	Open Awareness	Relaxation & Focus & Clarity	Beginner's mind	Planning	Performance Breaks
7	Open Awareness	Relaxation & Focus & Clarity	Acceptance	Communication	Commuting
8	Open Awareness	Change	Balance	Creativity	Emotional Balance
9	Open Awareness	Happiness	Joy	Change	Work-Life Balance
10	Open Awareness	Potential	Letting Go		
∞	Optional	All Qualities & Insights	Your Choice	Your Choice	

But keep in mind, both types of training are equally valuable and essential for a well-trained mind. There's value in continuing both.

During the ten-week program, the mental strategies are introduced one at a time, week after week. Although I recommend incorporating a new strategy each week, you may find that you want to spend more time with a particular strategy. Feel free to move from one strategy to the next at your own pace. And at the end of the ten weeks, you can choose a new strategy every day or every week.

By this point, you've likely experimented with many—or all—of the workplace techniques in Part I of the book. The final piece in implementing a ten-week training program is to choose a technique or two each week to actively focus on during your workday or while at home.

For example, try taking care of all your e-mail in two or three planned sessions per day as discussed in the technique on e-mails. Then try turning off all screened devices like smartphones, tablets, and televisions an hour before bedtime as recommended in the technique on how to improve sleep. It's through this type of more informal practice that you'll see and realize the natural benefits of the learnings and practices of mindfulness. And unlike your more formal ten-minute training sessions, it's simply having an intention to bring a special awareness into some of the activities that you already do on a daily basis.

To help you schedule each week of your self-guided training, I've included a simple, reproducible worksheet—called the Self-Guided Training Worksheet—in the appendix. There are also additional books and resources listed in the appendix that you'll find useful as you explore the best ways to integrate a more formal training program into your everyday life. Please use these resources as both motivation and support as you seek to improve your focus, clarity, and results.

Recognizing Progress

Maintaining training discipline is helped by experiencing progress. While the speed of progress differs among individuals and is difficult to put into simple metrics like percentages, the following five-point scale gives you an idea of your general progress:

1. Poor concentration and awareness. Only a few moments of clear focus on breath.
2. Primarily distracted. Periods of clear focus more frequent.
3. Equal balance between clear focus and distractions.
4. Stable concentration and awareness.
5. Strong concentration and clear awareness.

This incremental development of focus and awareness is beneficial not only during formal mindfulness training but also carries over into daily life. It makes you more present with the ones you care about and more effective in your activities because you're strengthening the neural networks of your brain. This is important to keep in mind: mindfulness is an active intervention in changing the neural networks of your brain. As you practice, it gets easier. As you practice, you'll be better able to face circumstances openly and directly: you'll be better at responding rather than reacting to experiences. With an enthusiastic and disciplined daily training, it's possible to reach the fourth or fifth level of the previous five-point scale within six months.

In the final section of this chapter, I'll cover some key success factors for bringing mindfulness into an organization. Hopefully, if you've made it to this point in the book, you're not only inspired to practice mindfulness for yourself but you're also interested in sharing it with your colleagues and organization.

Taking It into the Organization

Up to this point, the themes we've explored in this book have focused on you. We've looked in depth at the potential benefits of applying mindfulness for your own success and well-being. Since organizations are merely collections of busy individuals just like you, I hope you'll look to apply these strategies and guidelines toward increasing mindfulness throughout your organization. In truth, being the only mindful person in an organization can be lonely and frustrating. It can feel like you're enjoying benefits others are missing. This drives many people to become champions for mindfulness and to share it with others. If these methods and tools can help you be more efficient and productive, just imagine the potential if mindfulness were embraced by an entire team, division, or organization.

The measured benefits of corporate mindfulness initiatives are numerous, including increased focused, enhanced awareness, improved productivity, higher job satisfaction, enhanced creativity, reduced absenteeism, and reduced stress. Further, study after study suggests that mindfulness improves employees' overall sense of health and satisfaction. These are all terrific reasons to share the practices of mindfulness with others around you or within your organization. Based on years of experience in implementing corporate-based mindfulness programs, the following sections explain five key success factors for bringing mindfulness into an organization. The first major step is gaining leadership support.

Leadership Support

Any significant organizational initiative requires leadership support. If leaders are not onboard, individuals may benefit from mindfulness, but the organization is unlikely to become more mindful. And as with any successful change initiative, leaders need to lead by example. A leader that says she or he supports a mindfulness program but doesn't attend the sessions, or doesn't support group training, or is a constant source of distraction for employees will be sending mixed messages that weaken the initiative and confuse people throughout the organization.

This brings to mind an important distinction: when pursuing this type of support, it may be tempting to tell yourself, "I just need my boss's backing on this." But it often goes deeper than that. There are both formal and informal leaders within an organization. These informal leaders are often the influencers who aren't easily identified by title or salary and don't necessarily match up to the organizational chart. You need to be sure to know who these key people are and to build relationships with them. Who makes decisions that can affect you? Who has seniority? Who's politically connected within the office? Who do other people listen to in the lunch room or around the proverbial water cooler?

To successfully implement any program that may meet initial resistance, you need as much support, direction, and connectivity as possible. Identifying influencers and working to get as many of them as you can vested and committed is critical to success. This doesn't mean a leader or an influencer needs to attend every session or be 100 percent mindful in every moment. They do, however, need to have the focus and awareness to see how their behavior impacts others.

There are a couple of reasons this type of support and buy-in are so important. The first is what many people call "top cover." Simply put, top cover is protection from above. By communicating with leaders, you're building trust. They become invested in your success and the success of your proposed initiative. This can help you withstand any controversy around implementing a possibly misunderstood program like mindfulness into the office.

Another important reason why management needs to actively participate is that corporate mindfulness triggers a lot of key questions and discussions about the organization's working culture. How do we manage interruptions? How do we minimize distractions in meetings? How can we increase work-life balance? If leaders aren't actively involved, it limits the positive change that can come from these discussions.

Garnering this level of support requires building a trusting relationship based on the understanding that you're not trying to undermine or diminish anyone's authority. Instead, you're opening lanes of communication to gain beneficial insight and improve performance throughout the organization. You should make leadership feel as if by following your suggestions, they could become more effective leaders. Truly good leaders want to know how business assets are being developed and maintained: they want to know how to optimize their resources and cultivate departmental talent. One of the best ways to build this kind of trust and articulate the advantages of a corporate-based mindfulness program is to link it to broader organizational objectives.

Link to Organizational Objectives

Although there are tremendous benefits for training in mindfulness from an individual perspective, if the objective is to create a more mindful organization the initiative has to be linked to organizational objectives and goals. Mindfulness is not a panacea or magic pill that guarantees corporate success. But it is a means of increasing attention, focus, and productivity—all attributes that directly affect the bottom line of any organization.

Much of an initiative's success, therefore, depends on the ability to directly tie the personal benefits of mindfulness to tangible outcomes for the organization. This often means linking mindfulness and its many benefits to your organization's mission, to its long-term strategy, and to its shorter-term tactics. This may include explicitly explaining the business benefits of mindfulness—not that it will make people feel better or sleep better, but that it will result in fewer sick days and increased productivity, meaning lower costs, and higher revenue.

Doing so will not only help set priorities for a mindfulness initiative but it will also give you a clearer focus when formulating questions and preparing to meet with stakeholders. This, in turn, will convey the fact that you're diligent and attentive to the organization's larger needs, which will help lay the foundation for a program.

For example, an American construction company we worked with had four key corporate values: productivity, safety, customers, and employees. The CEO's primary interest in bringing mindfulness into his organization was to enhance the health and well-being of all employees. Other members of the senior leadership team were more interested in how training the mind could enhance productivity, safety, and perhaps even how people engaged with customers. Therefore, the specific objectives of the program were defined to include all of these key objectives—directly linked to the core strategy of the organization.

Effective Communication

As trendy as mindfulness appears to be right now, it's still a new concept in an organizational context. The idea of taking time out during a busy work day to sit in stillness for any period of time sounds a little odd at best and completely irrational at worst. This means it's important to provide clear and effective communication about the program: whom it's for, why it's seen as being valuable, and why people should consider giving it a try.

The word mindfulness itself can raise concerns about something spiritual or flaky, causing immediate skepticism and resistance. In this case, it's better to avoid the word when promoting an initiative. For example, at a global American technology company based in Asia, the program was called "Harnessing the Mind's Potential at Work," and the focus was on team effectiveness and enhancing collaboration. At a Canadian energy company, the program was named "Situational Awareness," and the objectives were enhancing environmental health and safety on-site in northern Alberta. In a number of our leadership programs, including one with a large financial services Company in Europe, the program is called "Sustainable Leadership Performance."

The point is, don't get stuck on the name or focus of the program. Instead, figure out what terminology best fits your organization's culture and objectives. This will allay any initial misunderstanding about or resistance to the program, as well as make it significantly easier to secure the next factor.

Time and Commitment

Mindfulness is not a quick fix. The many positive results that the method offers don't come out of thin air. It requires both individual and organizational investment to attain results. Specifically, it requires time and commitment. Individual habits take time to change, and collective habits take even longer. If you want an organization to benefit from mindfulness, it's effective if the effort is spread over a longer period of time than just one day or one week. This is the reason successful corporate-based mindfulness programs generally take place over four months, with a number of bite-sized, in-house workshops and daily training.

Building leadership support, linking the initiative to specific corporate objectives, and incorporating effective communication provide a solid foundation for gaining this type of commitment. Based on my experience in working with organizations that have successfully implemented mindfulness programs, getting many of these details settled up front has an enormous payoff in terms of realizing many of the benefits of corporate mindfulness. There is, however, one more factor critical to bringing mindfulness into any larger group.

Be the Change You Want to See

Mindfulness is a way of being. It's a way of showing up in life with kindness, openness, and presence. The best way to make others see the benefits of these qualities is to be them yourself. The kinder, more open, and more present you are, the more others will notice. And once they notice, they'll want to have the same demeanor you have. They'll aspire to feel the same peace and well-being you enjoy. I've seen it everywhere I've trained and taught—mindfulness is contagious.

If you'd like to get your organization to consider corporate mindfulness training, the very best piece of advice I can give you is to be mindful rather than to preach mindfulness.

Closing the Circle

The world is changing. We're getting bigger houses, better cars, and smarter phones. But does it make us happier? I don't think so. Happiness is an inner journey. The workshop is the mind. And mindfulness is the first step.

By taking time for this book, you've started a change within yourself. This took an investment of both your time and your money. To help sustain momentum during this change, I encourage you to choose at least three things from the book that have inspired you and follow through on them. Switch off the autopilot; be present with your colleagues, your friends, or your loved ones; and make space for the best version of yourself. Most important, try to maintain your daily practice.

That's where it all begins.

Of course, I know this is much easier said than done in our world of constant disruption and instant gratification, but it is worth the effort, because mindfulness makes us happier and kinder. Also, happy, kind people make for happier and kinder societies. I have personally experienced this for the past two decades and seen it in the changes in thousands of individuals and numerous organizations. You can do the same. When you fall off the horse—when you forget to train or get too busy to sit in the morning—remember that you can always get back up again.

Mindfulness is within you—if only you invite it.

And if on your mindfulness journey, you have a story you'd like to share, please let me know. Perhaps your story, like many in this book, will serve to inspire and motivate others on their mindfulness journey. You can e-mail me at rasmus.hougaard@potentialproject.com or introduce yourself if we're ever lucky enough to cross paths. I wish you all the best.

Acknowledgments

This book has come into the existence only by the kindness of people wiser than my coauthors and I. We are standing on the shoulders of giants in mind training, science, and business.

This book is dedicated to the masters who have taught me with love and generosity to manage my mind and to put others first, including the Dalai Lama, Lama Zopa Rinpoche, Lama Yeshe, Lakha Lama, Yangsi Rinpoche, Alan Wallace, Matthieu Ricard, Venerable Antonio Satta, Stephan Pende, Nyingje Chichester, Venerable Charles, and the venerable Michael Yeshe.

Many fantastic researchers have inspired and supported our work in The Potential Project. There are too many to mention here. In particular, we owe gratitude to Jochen Reb, Daniel Siegel, Jeremy Hunter, Richard Davidson, and Paul Ekman.

Enlightened people from organizations around the world have contributed to the creation of our organization and training program. There are too many to mention, but special thanks goes to Loren Shuster, Manish Chopra, Kenneth Egelund Schmidt, Christian Stadil, Adam Engle, and Jesper Askjaer.

I will be forever grateful to *all* my loved colleagues in The Potential Project. They have all been part of creating our program and thereby this book. Thank you brothers and sisters—and in particular, Jacqueline, Gillian, Erick, Martin, Wolfgang, John, Jude, and Jane.

This book has gone from good to great by the masterful minds of our editors at Benson-Collister Publishing Solutions, Jeff Leeson, and Rachel Livsey, as well as Nic Albert and Julie Kerr. Thank you so much. Also to Laurie Harting our amazing editor from Palgrave who really understands what we are about.

This book is dedicated to the families of my coauthors: Mark, Ben, Cam, Nick, Steve, Zack, James and Dan, and to my own wonderful family: my wife, Caroline, my daughter, Florien, my sons, Joris and Emil, and my parents, sister, and brother.

RASMUS HOUGAARD

Appendix: Self-Directed Training Resources

Self-Guided Training Worksheet

Week: _____

Foundational Practice: _____

Quality/Insight: _____

Mental Strategy: _____

Workplace Technique: _____

Notes: _____

_____

_____

_____

Choose one from each of the following categories:

- Foundational Practices: Sharp Focus, Open Awareness, Focused Awareness
- Qualities/Insights: Relaxation, Relaxation & Focus, Relaxation & Focus & Clarity, Change, Happiness, Potential
- Mental Strategies: Presence, Patience, Kindness, Beginner's Mind, Acceptance, Balance, Joy, Letting Go
- Workplace Technique: E-mails, Meetings, Goals, Priorities, Planning, Communication, Creativity, Managing Change, Mental Energy, Sleep, Eating & Energy, Energy & Activity, Performance Breaks, Commuting, Emotional Balance, Work-Life Balance

Appendix 1.1 QR code for LinkedIn discussion forum

Additional Resources

On bringing mindfulness to your organization: www.potentialproject. com

Find us and get regular news via LinkedIn, Facebook, and Twitter. Questions: mail@potentialproject.com

Your Training App

It's our hope the book has inspired you to take up a daily training. To make things easier for you, The Potential Project has developed a training app that will help you on your way. The app includes eight guided sessions of the foundational trainings described in this book. Also it gives you input on the mental strategies and reminders for regular performance breaks and more. To download the app, go to your preferred app store and search for "Potential Project Mindfulness."

Good Reads on Mindfulness

Mindfulness in Plain English by Bhante Henepola Gunaratana, 2002

Minding Closely: The Four Applications of Mindfulness by Alan Wallace, 2011

Wherever You Go, There You Are by John Kabat-Zinn, 2005

Why Meditate?: Working with Thoughts and Emotions, Mathieu Ricard, 2010

Peace Is Every Step: The Path of Mindfulness in Everyday Life by Thich Nhat Hanh, 1992

Mindfulness: A Practical Guide to Awakening by Joseph Goldstein, 2013

Good Reads on Mental Effectiveness at Work

Your Brain at Work: Strategies for Overcoming Distraction, Regaining Focus and Working Smarter All Day Long by David Rock, 2009

Focus: The Hidden Driven of Excellence by Daniel Goleman, 2013

Presence: Exploring Profound Change in People, Organizations, and Society by Peter Senge and Otto Scharmer, 2007

Search inside Yourself by Chade Meng Tan, 2012

Good Reads on the Science of Training the Mind

Mindsight: The New Science of Personal Transformation by Dan Siegel, 2010

Buddha's Brain: The Practical Neuroscience of Happiness, Love and Wisdom by Rick Hanson, 2009

The Emotional Life of Your Brain: How Its Unique Patterns Affect the Way You Think, Feel and Live by Richard J. Davidson and Sharon Begley, 2012

The Brain That Changes Itself: Stories of Personal Triumph from the Frontiers of Brain Science by Norman Doidge, 2007

Good Reads on Mindfulness at Work

Mindful Work: How Meditation Is Changing Business from the Inside Out by David Gelles, 2015

Working with Mindfulness: Mindfulness Work and Stress Reduction by Mirabai Bush and Daniel Goleman, 2013

Finding the Space to Lead: A Practical Guide to Mindful Leadership by Janice Maturano, 2013

The Mindful Leader: Ten Principles for Bringing Out the Best in Ourselves and Others by Michael Carrol, 2011

Mindfulness and Meditation Retreats

Reading a book is good. Doing the practice is great. There are many great places around the world where mindfulness retreats are offered by qualified teachers. Often these places will have a spiritual approach, mostly inspired from Buddhism. If that is the case, you are likely to be in good hands.

For local recommendations on retreat places, please contact our local offices via our website. You will find good people who are happy to help you.

A few venues and organizations that we like to recommend are:

- Multiversity in California. Hosting numerous great teachers and programs. 1440multiversity.org
- Garrison Institute in New York. Hosting numerous great teachers and programs. garrisoninstitute.org
- Thanyapura Mind Centre in Thailand. Hosting numerous great teachers and programs. Thanyapura.com/mind-centre
- Plum Village, France. Mindfulness retreats for individuals, groups and families. Plumvillage.org
- Goenka Vipassana retreats. A traditional ten-day deep dive into the practice. Offered locally across the globe. Dhamma.org

Notes

Introduction

1. Derek Dean and Caroline Webb (2012) "Recovering from Information Overload," *McKinsey Quarterly*, January.
2. E. M. Hallowell (2005) "Overloaded Circuits: Why Smart People Underperform," *Harvard Business Review*, January: 55–62.
3. Viktor E. Frankl, *Man's Search For Meaning* (Beacon Press, 1959),

1 Workplace Techniques

1. C. J. L. Murray and A. D. Lopez (1996), "Evidence Based Health Policy: Lessons from the Global Burden of Disease Study," *Science* Vol. 274, No. 5288: 740–743.

1 Mastering Your Mind—First Steps

1. M. A. Killingsworth and D. T. Gilbert (2010), "A Wandering Mind Is an Unhappy Mind," *Science 12*, Vol. 330, No. 6006: 932.
2. T. H. Davenport and J. C. Beck (2001), *The Attention Economy: Understanding the New Currency of Business* (Boston, MA: Harvard Business Review Press).
3. Killingsworth and Gilbert, "A Wandering Mind," 932.
4. Eyal Ophir, Clifford Nass, and Anthony D. Wagner. (2009), "Cognitive Control in Media Multitaskers," *Proceedings of the National Academy of Sciences of the United States of America)*, Vol. 106, No. 37: 15583–15587.
5. D. Bawden and L. Robinson (2009), "The Dark Side of Information: Overload, Anxiety and Other Paradoxes and Pathologies," *Journal of Information Science*, Vol. 25, No. 2: 180–191.
6. T. M. Amabile, C. N. Hadley and S. J. Kramer (2002), "Time Pressure and Creativity in Organizations—A Longitudinal Field Study," *Harvard Business School Working Paper*, No. 02–073.
7. S. Shellenbarger (2003), "New Studies Show Pitfalls of Doing Too Much at Once," *The Wall Street Journal*, February 27, wsj.com/articles/SB1046286576946413103.
8. E. M. Hallowell and J. J. Ratey (2006), *Delivered from Distraction—Getting the Most Out of Life with Attention Deficit Disorder* (New York: Ballantine Books).
9. R. J. Davidson et al. (2003), "Alterations in Brain and Immune Function Produced by Mindfulness Meditation," *Psychosomatic Medicine*, Vol. 65, No. 4: 564–570.

10. S. Rosenzweig, D. K. Reibel, J. M. Greeson, J. S. Edman, S. A. Jasser, K. D. McMearty, and B. J. Goldstein (2007), "Mindfulness-Based Stress Reduction Is Associated with Improved Glycemic Control in Type 2 Diabetes Mellitus," *Alternative Therapies in Health and Medicine*, Vol. 13, No. 5: 36–38.

11. F. Zeidan, S. K. Johnson, N. S. Gordon, and P. Goolkasian (2010), "Effects of Brief and Sham Mindfulness Meditation on Mood and Cardiovascular Variables," *Journal of Alternative and Complementary Medicine*, Vol. 16, No. 8: 867–873. Some research even suggests that mindfulness training slows the aging of the body at the cellular level. T. L. Jacobs et al. (2010), "Intensive Meditation Training, Immune Cell Telomerase Activity, and Psychological Mediators," *Psychoneuroendocrinology*, Vol. 36, No. 5: 664–681.

12. L. E. Carlson and S. N. Garland (2005), "Impact of Mindfulness Based Stress Reduction (MBSR) on Sleep, Mood, Stress and Fatigue Symptoms in Cancer Outpatients," *International Journal on Behavioral Medicine*, Vol. 12, No. 4: 278–285.

13. Christian G. Jensen, "Corporate-Based Mindfulness Training in Denmark—Three Validation Studies," Neurobiological Research Unit, Copenhagen University Hospital (forthcoming).

14. G. Pagnoni and M. Cekic (2007), "Age Effects on Gray Matter Volume and Attentional Performance," *Neurobiology of Aging*, Vol., 28, No. 10: 1623–1627.

15. F. Zeidan, S. K. Johnson, B. Diamond, Z. David, and P. Goolkasian (2010), "Mindfulness Meditation Improves Cognition—Evidence of Brief Mental Training," *Consciousness and Cognition*, Vol. 19, No. 2: 597–605.

16. K. A. MacLean et al. (2010) "Intensive Meditation Training Improves Perceptual Discrimination and Sustained Attention," *Psychological Science*, Vol. 21, No. 6: 829–839.

17. J. Greenberg, K. Reiner, and N. Meiran (2012), "Mind the Trap: Mindfulness Practice Reduces Cognitive Rigidity," *PLoS ONE*, 7(5): e36206.

18. Greenberg, Reiner, and Meiran, "Mind the Trap," e36206.

19. Zeidan et al., "Effects of Brief and Sham Mindfulness Meditation."

20. Based on research by Professor Jochen Reb of Singapore Management University of CBMT programs at Carlsberg and If Insurance. At the time of publication, these results had been presented at conferences but not yet published. You can see presentations of some of the results at www.youtube.com/potentialproject and find the results published at www.potentialproject.com from the end of 2013. A researcher from the University of Copenhagen found similar benefits from his evaluation of a nine-week program at a private hospital in Copenhagen. Jensen, "Corporate-Based Mindfulness Training in Denmark."

21. M. Murphy and S. Donovan (1999), *The Physical and Psychological Effects of Meditation: A Review of Contemporary Research with a Comprehensive Bibliography, 1931–1996* (2nd ed.) (Sausalito, CA: Institute of Noetic Sciences).

22. T. L. Giluk (2010), "Mindfulness-Based Stress Reduction: Facilitating Work Outcomes through Experienced Affect and High-Quality Relationships," PhD diss., University of Iowa.

23. B. Barrett, M. S. Hayney, D. Muller, D. Rakel, A. Ward, C. N. Obasi, R. Brown, Z. Zhang, A. Zgierska, J. Gern, R. West, T. Ewers, S. Barlow, M. Gassman, and C. L. Coe (2012), "Meditation or Exercise for Preventing Acute Respiratory Infection: A Randomized Controlled Trial," *Annals of Family Medicine*, Vol. 10, No. 4: 337–346.

24. S. L. Shapiro, H. Jazaieri, and P. Goldin (2012), "Mindfulness-Based Stress Reduction Effects on Moral Reasoning and Decision Making," *Journal of Positive Psychology*, Vol. 7, No. 6: 504–515.

Technique #1   E-mails

1. The Radicati Group, Inc. (2011), E-mail Statistics Report, www.radicati.com/?p=7261; Pew Internet, www.pewinternet.org.
2. The Radicati Group, Inc., E-mail Statistics Report.
3. The Radicati Group, Inc., E-mail Statistics Report.
4. M. Koneya and A. Barbour (1976), *Louder Than Words…Nonverbal Communication* (New York: Merrill).

Technique #2   Meetings

1. R. Williams (2012), "How Meetings Kill Productivity," *Financial Post*, April 18, business.financialpost.com/2012/04/18/how-meetings-kill-productivity.
2. L. Belkin (2007), "Time Wasted? Perhaps It's Well Spent," *The New York Times*, May 31, www.nytimes.com/2007/05/31/fashion/31work.html.
3. http://www.bcbusiness.ca/lifestyle/bryan-dysons-30-second-speech.

Technique #4   Priorities

1. K. Kogon, A. Merrill, and L. Rinne (2015), *The 5 Choices: The Path to Extraordinary Productivity* (New York: Simon & Schuster).
2. H. Bruch and S. Ghoshal (2002), "Beware the Busy Manager," *Harvard Business Review*, February.

Technique #6   Communication

1. https://en.wikiquote.org/wiki/Alan_Greenspan

Technique #7   Creativity

1. K. H. Kim (2011), "The Creativity Crisis: The Decrease in Creative Thinking Scores on the Torrance Tests of Creative Thinking," *Creativity Research Journal*, Vol. 23, Issue 4: 285–295.
2. V. Capurso, F. Fabbro, and C. Crescentini (2013), "Mindful Creativity: The Influence of Mindfulness Meditation on Creative Thinking," *Frontiers in Psychology*, Vol. 4: 1020.
3. https://en.wikipedia.org/wiki/Hans_Hofmann.
4. T. M. Amabile, J. S. Mueller, W. B. Simpson, C. N. Hadley, S. J. Kramer and L.Fleming (2002), "Time Pressure and Creativity in Organizations—A Longitudinal Field Study," *Harvard Business School Working Paper*: No. 02–073.

Technique #8   Change

1. David Hamilton (2005), *Social Cognition: Key Readings* (New York: Psychology Press),

Technique #9   Mental Energy

1. John Ding-E Young and Eugene Taylor (1998), "Meditation as a Voluntary Hypometabolic State of Biological Estivation," *American Physiological Society*, Issue 13: 149–153, http://www.ncbi.nlm.nih.gov/pubmed/11390779.

2. Matthew A. Killingsworth and Daniel T. Gilbert (2010), "A Wandering Mind Is an Unhappy Mind," *Science 12*, Vol. 330, No. 6006: 932.

Technique #10 Enhancing Sleep

1. John Medina (2008), *Brain Rules* (Seattle: Pear Press).
2. Linda E. Carlson (2005), "Impact of Mindfulness Based Stress Reduction (MBSR) on Sleep, Mood, Stress and Fatigue Symptoms in Cancer Outpatients," *International Journal on Behavioral Medicine*, Vol. 12, No. 4: 278–285.
3. A. Brzezinski (1997), "Melatonin in Humans," *The New England Journal of Medicine*, 336: 186–195.
4. Brzezinski, "Melatonin in Humans."
5. M. G. Figueiro, B. Wood, B. Plitnick, and M. S. Rea (2011), "The Impact of Light from Computer Monitors on Melatonin Levels in College Students," *Neuro Endocrinology Letters*, Vol. 32, No. 2: 158–163.
6. J. C. Pruessner, O. T. Wolf, D. H. Hellhammer, A. Buske-Kirschbaum, K. van Auer, S. Jobst, F. Kaspers, and C. Kirschbaum (1997), "Free Cortisol Levels after Awakening," *Life Science Journal*, Vol. 61, No. 26: 2539–2549.

Technique #11 Eating and Energy

1. Brian Wansink (2010), "From Mindless Eating to Mindlessly Eating Better," *Physiology & Behavior*, Vol. 100: 454–463.
2. Robert E. Thayer (1987), "Energy, Tiredness, and Tension Effects of a Sugar Snack Versus Moderate Exercise," *Journal of Personality and Social Psychology*, Vol. 52, No. 1: 119–125.

Strategy #1 The Power of Presence

1. E. M. Hallowell (January 2005), "Overloaded Circuits: Why Smart People Underperform," *Harvard Business Review*: 55–62.
2. Hallowell, "Overloaded Circuits."
3. Hallowell, "Overloaded Circuits."
4. Hallowell, "Overloaded Circuits."

Strategy #2 Patience

1. P. D. MacLean (1990), *The Triune Brain in Evolution—Role in Paleocerebral Functions* (New York: Plenum Press); S. T. Robin, I. M. Dunbar, and S. Shultz (2007), "Evolution in the Social Brain," *Science*, Vol. 317, No. 5843: 1344–1347.

Strategy #3 Kindness

1. J. Vahtera, M. Kivimaki, A. Uutela, J. Pentti (2000), "Hostility and Ill Health: Role of Psychosocial Resources in Two Contexts of Working Life," *Journal of Psychosomatic Research*, Vol. 48, Issue 1: 89–98.
2. G. Rein, M. Atkinson and R. McCraty. (1995), "The Physiological and Psychological Effects of Compassion and Anger," *Journal of Advancement in Medicine*, Vol. 8, No. 2: 87–105.

3. C. Peterson, N. Park and M. E. P. Seligman et al. (2005), "Orientations to Happiness and Life Satisfaction: The Full Life vs. the Empty Life," *Journal of Happiness Studies*, Vol. 6: 25–41.

Strategy #4   Beginner's Mind

1. Ann M. Graybiel (1998), "The Basal Ganglia and Chunking of Action Repertoires," *Neurology of Learning and Memory*, Vol. 70; Charles Duhigg (2012), *The Power of Habit*, New York: Random House.
2. J. Greenberg, K. Reiner, and N. Meiran (2012), "Mind the Trap: Mindfulness Practice Reduces Cognitive Rigidity," *PLOS*, DOI: 10.1371/journal.pone.0036206.

Strategy #6   Balance

1. Tor Nørretranders: *Mærk Verden—En beretning om bevidsthed* [Notice the world—a report about consciousness] (2000), (Copenhagen: Gyldendal).
2. Y. Xinjun, M. Fumoto, Y. Nakatani, T. Sekiyama, H. Kikuchi, Y. Seki, I. Sato-Suzuki, and H. Arita (2011), "Activation of the Anterior Prefrontal Cortex and Serotonergic System Is Associated with Improvements in Mood and EEG Changes Induced by Zen Meditation Practice in Novices," *International Journal of Psychophysiology*, Vol. 80, No. 2: 103–111; B. K. Hölzel, J. Carmody, M. Vangel, C. Congleton, S. M. Yerramsetti, T. Gard, and S. W. Lazar (2011), *Psychiatry Research: Neuroimaging*, Vol. 191: 36–43.

Strategy #7   Joy

1. B. L. Fredrickson (2003), "The Value of Positive Emotions," *American Scientist*, Vol. 91: 330–335.
2. J. Fowler and N. Christakis (2008), "Dynamic Spread of Happiness in a Large Social Network: Longitudinal Analysis over 20 Years in the Framingham Heart Study," *British Medical Journal*, Vol. 337, No. a2338, doi:10.1136.
3. D. Lohmar (2006), "Mirror Neurons and the Phenomenology of Intersubjectivity," *Phenomenology and the Cognitive Sciences*, Vol. 5, No. 1: 5–16.

2   Training Sharp Focus

1. Based on research by Professor Jochen Reb from Singapore Management University of CBMT programs at Carlsberg and If Insurance. At the time of going to press these results have been presented at conferences but not yet published. You can see presentations of some of the results at www.youtube.com/potentialproject and find the results published at www.potentialproject.com from around the end of 2013.
2. M. A. Killingsworth and D. T. Gilbert (2010), "A Wandering Mind Is an Unhappy Mind," *Science 12*, Vol. 330, No. 6006: 932.
3. Killingsworth and Gilbert, 932.

About the Authors

Rasmus Hougaard is an internationally recognized authority on training the mind to be more focused, effective, and clear in an organizational context. He is the founder and managing director of The Potential Project.

Rasmus's background combines research in organizational development with a corporate career and more than 20 years of practicing and teaching mindfulness. In 2008, after years of working with leading scientists, corporate executives, and mind training experts, Rasmus launched The Potential Project. The mission of The Potential Project is to contribute to a more peaceful world by helping individuals, teams, and organizations become kinder, wiser, and more effective in everything they do.

Through the work of The Potential Project, Rasmus has helped organizations like Microsoft, Accenture, Roche, Nike, American Express, General Electric, Citrix, Google, Sony, Société Générale, KLM, IKEA, Royal Bank of Canada, Ogilvy, Carlsberg, and many more develop organizational excellence, and helped thousands of individuals lead happier, kinder, and more effective work lives.

Rasmus is a sought-after keynote speaker at international conferences, workshops, and seminars around the world. He's also a guest speaker at numerous universities and business schools like Cranfield Business School, Rotman Business School, ESSEC Business School, Singapore Management University, and Copenhagen Business School.

Jacqueline Carter has over 20 years of consulting and management experience helping organizations enhance performance, manage change and achieve results. She is passionate about helping individuals and organizations realize their potential through training the mind. She is a partner of The Potential Project International and director of The Potential Project North America. Her clients include Google, Sony, American Express, Royal Bank of Canada, and Suncor, to name a few. Jacqueline is a contributor to the *Huffington Post* and has appeared on Channel News Asia Breakfast Television, as well as radio talk shows. She is an engaging and energizing speaker and has conducted key-notes and led workshops at conferences and leading business schools around the world.

Gillian Coutts has over 20 years of experience as a leader and change agent in the sales and operations functions of large corporations. She has worked across a range of industries, including retail, government, transport, oil and gas, and human services. Gillian is a partner with The Potential Project Australia. Her clients include Yahoo!7, Telstra, Suncorp, and large not-for-profit organizations. She also sits on a number of boards and regularly speaks on integrating mindfulness into leadership, work life, and—following her own wake-up call of cancer diagnosis and treatment—programs for posttraumatic growth.

About The Potential Project

The Potential Project is the global leading provider of mindfulness-based training solutions for organizations. With offices in more than 20 countries in North America, Europe, Asia, Australia, and New Zealand, and a client list including Microsoft, Accenture, Roche, Nike, American Express, General Electric, Citrix, Google, Sony, Société Générale, KLM, IKEA, Royal Bank of Canada, Ogilvy, and Carlsberg, The Potential Project positively impacts organizational excellence as well as the lives of thousands individuals. In 2014, they trained more than 25,000 people, and the number increases year after year.

The mission of The Potential Project is to contribute to a more peaceful world by helping individuals, teams, and organizations become kinder, wiser, and more effective in everything they do.

The work of The Potential Project is delivered as face-to-face or online training solutions based on the methods in this book and always tailored to each specific client. Their offerings include a product range starting at the introductory level and moving into in-depth cultural interventions for leaders, teams, or individual employees.

While The Potential Project was founded by Rasmus Hougaard, its Corporate-Based Mindfulness Training program was developed by leading experts in mind training, science, and business, and defines the global gold standard in mindfulness in organizations. The program is undergoing constant scientific research by researchers at leading universities and business schools.

If you are interested in a conversation on how you can bring mindfulness training into your organization, you can find contact details for local trainers in your area at potentialproject.com.

Illustrations

Figures

Table

Index